FORGIVING PEOPLE WHO REJECT YOU

21 Day Journal To Heal The Wounds, Build Resilience, And Embrace Your Authentic Self

Blending Our Love, Maryland

Copyright © 2023 by Tuniscia Okeke

Published 2023

Library of Congress Cataloging-in-Publication Data

ISBN: 978-1-962748-14-8 (Print)

ISBN: 978-1-962748-15-5 (eBook)

Printed in the United States of America

FORGIVING PEOPLE WHO REJECT YOU

21 Day Journal To Heal The Wounds, Build Resilience, And Embrace Your Authentic Self

TUNISCIA OKEKE

BLENDING OUR LOVE, INC.

DEDICATION

To all the family and friends who rejected
me and taught me life's valuable lessons,

I dedicate this journal to you.

I extend my forgiveness and heartfelt gratitude.

Your presence in my journey helped me
learn the true essence of self-love.

Thank you.

TABLE OF CONTENTS

Paying It Forward 1

Foreword 5

Introduction : Unshackling The Heart 7

The Power Of Forgiveness 23

21 Benefits of a 21-Day Commitment 39

Day 1: I Forgive My Mind For Believing My Parents
Rejected Me 51

Day 2: I Forgive My Mind For Believing My Family
Rejects And Belittles My Creative Ideas 57

Day 3: I Forgive My Mind For Believing My Friends
Reject & Minimize My Business 63

Day 4: I Forgive The Rejection And Judgment In
Religious Spaces 69

Day 5: I Forgive Any Rejection From People Who
Left Me Emotionally Bruised 75

Day 6: I Forgive Co-Workers For Rejecting My
Kindness And Gossiping Behind My Back 81

Day 7: I Forgive My Peers For Rejecting Me By
Constantly Judging My Success 87

Day 8: I Forgive Society For Rejecting Me Due to
Their Unrealistic Expectations 93

Day 9: I Forgive My Mind For Judging People Who Decline
My Services And Internalizing It As A Rejection 99

Day 10: I Forgive Myself For The Self-Rejection 105

Day 11: I Forgive My Employer For Denying The
Promotion, Which I Took As A Rejection 113

Day 12: I Forgive All Of The Romantic Rejections 119

Day 13: I Forgive My Children For Their Rejection.......... 125

Day 14: I Forgive Any Teachers Who Belittled &
Insulted Me 131

Day 15: I Forgive People Online For Their Harsh
Judgment And Rejection 137

Day 16: I Forgive Those Who Reject Me Due To
Their Prejudices 143

Day 17: I Forgive Those Who Reject My Loved Ones........149

Day 18: I Forgive Those Who Reject & Undermine
My Femininity 155

Day 19: I Forgive The Rejection Motherhood Brings........161

Day 20: I Forgive Those Who Reject My Existence 169

Day 21: I Forgive Those Who Reject Me Due To
The Melanin In My Skin...175

Story Time 181

Embracing E & A... 185

Paying It Forward

I 'm sharing this message as the author of this 21-day journal on forgiveness, not just with words on these pages but with a story that has shaped my life's purpose. As I embark on this journey with you, I want to share the deeply personal and transformative experiences that led me to write, edit, and self-publish 35 journals on forgiveness in less than a year.

My forgiveness journey began when I was 24, a pivotal age when life often feels like an open book, brimming with hope and dreams. Then, my mother called me on a seemingly ordinary Monday morning, and with those words, she unraveled the narrative of my life. She revealed that the man I had believed to be my father for all those years was, in fact, not my biological father.

The weight of that revelation was crushing. It was as if the ground beneath me had shifted, leaving me unsteady and disoriented. But what shook me to my core was not the revelation itself but the sudden rupture of trust in my mother—the person I had always looked up to as a paragon of love, trustworthiness, and honesty.

In the wake of this revelation, I spiraled into a deep pit of resentment, anger, and pain. I grappled with a profound sense of betrayal and felt adrift in a sea of unanswered questions. It was a turbulent period in my life, and for 17 long years, I carried the heavy burden of unforgiveness.

Then, something remarkable happened that would alter the course of my life forever. I noticed a pattern in my relationship with my children. They treated me with a lack of respect and love, leaving me bewildered and hurt. In desperation, I turned to prayer one day, seeking answers from a higher source.

God's voice whispered into my heart in that sacred space of prayer and introspection, revealing a profound truth: "I taught them how to love me by the way I loved my mother."

Those words struck me like lightning, piercing through the fog of my confusion. It was an awakening—a profound realization that, in my quest for revenge against my mother, I had unwittingly passed on the energy of resentment to my children. I had normalized my hurtful behaviors as the way we should treat our mothers.

On my 40th birthday, I consciously confronted my soul's deepest and darkest corners. I embarked on a journey of healing, self-forgiveness, and forgiveness of my mother. My primary motivation was to restore my relationship with my children and teach them how to pass on healing, love, and forgiveness to their children.

That six-year odyssey of healing was transformative beyond measure. It led me to write 35 journals, each addressing a facet of forgiveness and healing I encountered on my journey. These journals became my way of reaching out to others grappling with their forgiveness journeys.

Today, I extend a heartfelt invitation to you to embark on this 21-day journey with me. Just as my healing journey began with a single journal, this journal can be your compass for forgiveness, healing, and growth.

I send you loving energy as you navigate through the complexities of your forgiveness journey, and I hope these pages serve as a guiding light toward wholeness and inner peace.

With love and compassion,

Tuniscia O

FOREWORD

Dear Beloved Readers,

I am deeply honored to guide you through the transformative journey of "Forgiving People Who Reject You: A 21-Day Journal." This journal is your sacred space, your companion on a path of inner healing, resilience-building, and self-discovery.

Within these pages, you'll find the tools and prompts to explore your inner world, confront the wounds of rejection, and embark on a profound journey of forgiveness. Each day is an opportunity to go inward, to untangle the complexities of your emotions, and to release the burdens of the past.

As the author, I want you to know that your healing matters deeply to me. I've walked a similar path, and I understand the courage it takes to confront past hurts. But in this journey, you'll find strength, resilience, and the authentic self you've always longed to embrace.

This journal is your sanctuary, your safe haven for self-reflection and growth. It's a testament to your commitment to healing and self-empowerment.

I invite you to embark on this 21-day adventure with an open heart and a willingness to forgive, heal, and rediscover your true self. Know that you are not alone; I am here with you in spirit every step of the way.

With boundless gratitude and warmest regards,

Tuniscia O

Unshackling The Heart

Introduction

H ealing is the unshackling of the heart when forgiving those who've rejected us. It's a profound liberation that frees us from the weight of resentment and hurt. Forgiveness unlocks our capacity for empathy and understanding, allowing us to see past the rejection's pain. As we release these emotional shackles, our hearts expand, mending the wounds of denial. It's in this release that we discover the transformative power of forgiveness. This force not only mends the past but also paves the way for a future filled with resilience, self-compassion, and the ability to embrace rejection as a catalyst for personal growth.

In the tapestry of our lives, we encounter a myriad of experiences and interactions that shape our beliefs, perceptions, and emotions. Among these experiences, few emotions cut as deeply as rejection. Whether it's the subtle brush-off from a friend, the harsh judgment of a stranger, or the dismissal by someone we hold dear, the sting of rejection can reverberate throughout our entire being.

This sacred journal is designed to guide you on a transformative journey toward healing, forgiveness, and empowerment. It is a journey that invites you to explore the layers of your emotions, confront the pain of rejection, and, ultimately, release its grip on your heart and soul. As you embark on this journey, know that you are not alone. Countless individuals have walked this path before you, and within these pages, you will find the tools, reflections, and affirmations to guide you through the process.

Explore the different forms rejection can take, from the subtlest dismissals to the most heart-wrenching betrayals. Through self-reflection exercises, you'll uncover how rejection has impacted your sense of self-worth, relationships, and overall well-being. Understanding the roots of these emotions lays the foundation for your journey toward healing.

Rejection, in all its multifaceted forms, is a universal human experience that has the power to shape our sense of self, relationships, and overall well-being. It's a complex emotion, often lurking in the shadows of our consciousness, influencing our decisions and actions profoundly. When embarking on a healing journey, dissecting the anatomy of rejection, understanding its various manifestations, and recognizing how it has impacted our lives is crucial.

Subtle Dismissals And Micro-Rejections

Rejection doesn't always come as a loud, unmistakable blow. It can be subtle, often manifesting as micro-rejections, small gestures, or dismissals that accumulate over time. These seemingly insignificant acts can erode our self-esteem and sense of belonging, leaving us with a lingering feeling of inadequacy.

Consider those times when you shared an idea that was met with indifference or silence. Or when you contacted a friend and they took days to respond. These tiny pricks of rejection can accumulate and fester, affecting our self-worth and leaving us hesitant to express ourselves.

Subtle dismissals and micro-rejections are the quiet but insidious cousins of rejection. They may seem like minor blips on life's radar, but their cumulative impact can be profound. These subtle gestures and dismissals, often overlooked or dismissed, can chip away at our self-esteem and sense of belonging.

Picture the moments when your contributions in a conversation were met with indifference or when your ideas were brushed aside without consideration. These seemingly trivial acts can slowly erode our self-worth, like water-wearing away a stone. Each micro-rejection leaves behind a trace of inadequacy, whispering to us that our thoughts and feelings don't matter.

Over time, this sense of not quite measuring up can manifest in various aspects of our lives. It can affect our confidence, making us hesitate to voice our opinions or share our talents. It can influence our relationships, causing us to question if we truly belong or are tolerated.

The challenge lies in recognizing these micro-rejections and their cumulative effect. Often, they're dismissed as hypersensitivity or overthinking. However, acknowledging their impact is the first step toward healing. It's about understanding that even subtle dismissals matter and have consequences.

In your journey of self-discovery and healing, reflect on these subtle dismissals. Recognize their influence on your self-esteem and sense of belonging. With this awareness, you can rebuild your self-worth, affirm your value, and find a place where you truly belong, free from the weight of accumulated micro-rejections.

Social Exclusion And Alienation

Rejection can take the form of social exclusion or alienation, where we are intentionally left out or made to feel like outsiders. It's the feeling of being on the fringe, looking in at social gatherings, workplaces, or even within families, where we feel like we don't quite belong.

The impact of social exclusion can be profound, leading to loneliness, isolation, and questioning our worthiness of connection. It often results in deep sadness and anxiety, further perpetuating our fears of rejection.

Social exclusion and alienation, forms of rejection in the social sphere, can cast a long shadow on our emotional well-being. The impact of being left out or made to feel like an outsider is profound, extending far beyond the moments of exclusion. These experiences can lead to a deep sense of loneliness, isolation, and questioning our worthiness of connection.

When excluded, it's as if a fundamental need for human connection is denied. Loneliness creeps in, and we may wonder what is wrong with us, why we don't fit in, or why we're not accepted. Questioning our worthiness can plant seeds of self-doubt, and a vicious cycle ensues.

The sadness that accompanies social exclusion is often accompanied by anxiety. We may become apprehensive about future social interactions, fearing more rejection. This anxiety can be crippling, challenging to engage in new relationships or maintain existing ones. It's a self-fulfilling prophecy; the fear of rejection can inadvertently push us further away from potential connection sources.

Social exclusion can become a heavy burden in this cycle, weighing on our self-esteem and mental health. Recognizing the emotional toll of exclusion is the first step toward healing. It's essential to understand that the actions or judgments of others do not determine our worthiness of connection. Embracing our authentic selves and seeking out supportive, inclusive communities can help break the cycle of loneliness and anxiety, offering a path to emotional healing and resilience.

Romantic Rejection And Heartbreak

One of the most poignant forms of rejection is romantic heartbreak. When someone we love ends a relationship or chooses another path, it can shatter our sense of self and security. The pain of unrequited love or a breakup can be excruciating, leaving emotional scars that take time to heal.

Romantic rejection can trigger feelings of unworthiness, abandonment, and a fear of future rejection in matters of the heart. It's a deep wound that can impact our ability to trust and open up to new relationships.

Romantic rejection and heartbreak, perhaps the most poignant forms, can leave deep emotional scars. When someone we deeply care about ends a relationship or chooses another path, it can devastate our self-worth and security.

We often grapple with feelings of unworthiness in the aftermath of romantic rejection. We question our value and what we may have lacked that led to the rejection. It's as if our self-esteem takes a severe hit, leaving us vulnerable to believing that we do not deserve love.

Furthermore, the sense of abandonment that accompanies heartbreak can be excruciating. We may feel cast aside, unimportant, and left to navigate a sea of emotions alone. It's a profound emotional wound that can intensify feelings of isolation and despair.

Perhaps most significantly, romantic rejection can trigger a fear of future rejection in matters of the heart. This fear can lead to emotional guardedness, making it difficult to trust and open up to new relationships. We may build walls around our hearts to protect ourselves from the possibility of being hurt again, unintentionally sabotaging our chances of forming meaningful connections.

Healing from romantic rejection takes time, self-compassion, and, often, professional support. It involves recognizing that any relationship or person's choices don't define our worth. It's about learning to trust ourselves again, rebuilding our self-esteem, and ultimately, allowing our hearts to mend and open up to the possibility of love again. While the emotional scars may linger, they can serve as a testament to our resilience and capacity for growth.

Betrayal And Trust Violations

A betrayal is a form of rejection striking at the core of our trust and security. It can occur in friendships, family relationships, or professional settings. Betrayal involves a breach of trust, where someone we rely on breaks that trust, often in a significant and painful way.

Experiencing betrayal can lead to a profound sense of hurt, anger, and disillusionment. It can shake our belief in the goodness of others and leave us questioning our judgment. The scars of betrayal can run deep and impact our ability to form meaningful connections in the future.

Betrayal and trust violations are like earthquakes in the landscape of our relationships, causing deep fault lines that rupture our sense of security and faith in others. The emotional wounds can be profound when someone we trust breaches that trust, whether through deceit, disloyalty, or dishonesty.

Betrayal often unleashes a storm of emotions. It's a complex mix of hurt, anger, and disillusionment. The pain of being betrayed by someone we believe in can be overwhelming, leaving us questioning our judgment. We may wonder how we could have been wrong about someone's true character or intentions.

Moreover, betrayal can shatter our belief in the inherent goodness of others. It's as if a mirror we held up to the world, reflecting our faith in humanity, has been cracked. This loss of trust in others can have far-reaching consequences, making it challenging to form new connections or trust in future relationships.

The scars of betrayal, much like the remnants of an earthquake, can run deep and persist for a long time. They can make us cautious and guarded, hindering our ability to open up emotionally or fully trust others again. Healing from betrayal involves processing these emotions, seeking closure if possible, and gradually rebuilding trust in others and our judgment. While the scars may remain, they can serve as a reminder of our resilience and capacity for growth, showing that even after a breach of trust, we can learn to trust and love again.

Story Time

Dana had always been a cautious soul when it came to trusting others. Betrayal and disappointment seemed to be recurring themes in her life, leaving her with deep-seated trust issues. She had learned to keep her expectations low, believing it was a way to protect herself from being hurt.

One day, Dana attended a conference on personal growth and self-improvement. It was here that she heard a speaker discussing the concept of accountability for one's thoughts and beliefs. The idea struck a chord with her, and she couldn't help but reflect on her own mindset.

During a moment of introspection, Dana realized that she had never truly had high expectations of people. She had always approached relationships with the anticipation of being let down, almost as if she were preparing herself for the inevitable heartbreak. Her belief in the goodness of others had been overshadowed by her fear of betrayal.

It was a pivotal moment for Dana. She recognized that her low expectations were not a form of protection but a self-fulfilling prophecy. She decided to take a chance and shift her mindset. What did she have to lose, after all? She had already experienced her fair share of heartache.

Dana began to approach her interactions with an open heart and a newfound belief in the goodness of people. She chose to give others the benefit of the doubt, even when her past experiences tempted her to do otherwise. It wasn't an instant transformation, but over time, something remarkable happened.

As Dana started to see the good in people and expect kindness rather than betrayal, her life began to change. She attracted friends and acquaintances who reciprocated her positivity. People responded to her newfound trust with warmth and authenticity.

Dana's world transformed from one of constant skepticism and guardedness to a place where she could truly connect with others. By shifting her belief and allowing herself to expect kindness, she not only rebuilt her trust in people but also rediscovered the beauty of genuine human connections. Dana's journey showed her that sometimes, taking a chance on trust could lead to the most remarkable transformations.

Self-Rejection And Negative Self-Talk

The most insidious form of rejection is self-rejection, where we internalize feelings of unworthiness and inadequacy. It's the harsh self-criticism, negative self-talk, and the belief that we are inherently flawed.

Self-rejection is a self-fulfilling prophecy; when we believe we do not deserve love or success, we often unconsciously sabotage our opportunities for growth and connection. It's essential to recognize and challenge this form of rejection to begin the journey of healing.

Remember that healing from rejection is a process that takes time and self-compassion. Understanding the anatomy of rejection and its impact on your life lays the foundation for your journey toward healing, resilience, and the ability to embrace your authentic self.

Self-rejection and negative self-talk are like invisible chains that bind our sense of self-worth. When we internalize unworthiness and inadequacy, we become our harshest critics, perpetuating a cycle of self-sabotage and emotional pain.

This rejection turns our thoughts into weapons, continually chipping away at our self-esteem. Negative self-talk manifests as an inner monologue of self-criticism, reminding us of our perceived flaws and mistakes. We begin to believe we are inherently flawed and undeserving of love, success, or happiness.

The impact of self-rejection and negative self-talk can be profound. It affects every aspect of our lives, from relationships to career choices. It can lead to self-imposed limitations, preventing us from pursuing goals or enjoying fulfilling relationships.

Understanding the anatomy of self-rejection is the first step towards healing. It involves recognizing negative self-talk patterns, challenging irrational beliefs, and learning to treat ourselves with self-compassion. Healing from self-rejection is a journey towards embracing our authentic selves, acknowledging our worthiness, and breaking free from the chains of self-criticism.

By laying this foundation for healing, we cultivate resilience and open the door to a life where self-love, self-acceptance, and a genuine embrace of our authentic selves can flourish.

Release Self-Rejection

Self-rejection can be a silent and insidious force that shapes how we perceive ourselves and allows others to treat us. It's a pattern that often starts within and can have far-reaching consequences in our relationships and overall well-being.

When we reject ourselves, we send a powerful message to our subconscious that we are not worthy of love, respect, or kindness. This self-inflicted wound can lead to a cascade of negative effects. One of the most significant consequences is that it normalizes allowing people to reject us in various aspects of their lives.

When we don't value ourselves, we set the bar low in our expectations of how others should treat us. We become accustomed to accepting the bare minimum from people, whether in respect, communication, or consideration. This normalization of low standards can lead to a cycle of unhealthy relationships where we tolerate mistreatment, belittling, or neglect.

Moreover, self-rejection can create a vicious cycle of seeking external validation and approval. We may find ourselves constantly trying to earn the love and acceptance of others, even if it means compromising our boundaries and self-respect. This need for validation can make us vulnerable to people who may exploit our desperation for approval.

Breaking free from this pattern of self-rejection requires self-awareness and a commitment to self-love and self-acceptance. It involves recognizing the negative beliefs we hold about ourselves and challenging them. It means setting healthy boundaries and refusing to accept mistreatment from others.

Ultimately, rejecting self-rejection is a powerful act of self-empowerment. It means recognizing our inherent worth and refusing to allow anyone, including ourselves, to undermine it. It's about reclaiming our self-esteem, setting higher standards for our treatment, and surrounding ourselves with people who uplift and respect us.

By rejecting self-rejection, we can break free from the cycle of normalizing mistreatment and embark on a journey of self-discovery and self-love. It's a transformative process that can lead to healthier, more fulfilling relationships and a greater sense of inner peace and happiness.

The Power Of Forgiveness

F orgiving those who have rejected you doesn't condone their actions; rather, it frees you from the chains of bitterness and resentment. You will learn about the transformative power of forgiveness for yourself and the people who have hurt you. Through thought-provoking questions and contemplative exercises, you will begin to unravel the knots of anger and resentment that have held you captive.

The power of forgiveness is a profound act of liberation. When you choose to forgive those who have rejected you, it's not a condonation of their actions; instead, it's a courageous step towards releasing yourself from the suffocating chains of bitterness and resentment.

Forgiveness is a gift you give to yourself, a declaration that you refuse to be held hostage by the pain of rejection. It's a conscious decision to reclaim your own peace and emotional well-being. By forgiving, you disentangle your worth from the hurtful actions of others.

Moreover, forgiveness is an acknowledgment of your inner strength. Extending grace to those who have caused you pain takes great courage. It's a testament to your resilience, demonstrating that you refuse to be defined by the wounds inflicted upon you.

Forgiveness doesn't erase the past or require you to forget. Instead, it allows you to transcend the pain, learn and grow from it, and forge a path toward healing and inner peace. It's a testament to your capacity for empathy, understanding, and compassion, even in rejection.

Ultimately, forgiveness empowers you to reclaim your narrative. It shifts the focus from the actions of others to your journey of healing and self-discovery. It's a declaration that you hold the power to shape your destiny, free from the weight of resentment. Through forgiveness, you enter a future defined by love, self-compassion, and the unshakable knowledge that you deserve belonging and acceptance.

Embracing Self-Compassion

Embracing self-compassion is the cornerstone of breaking free from the cycle of rejection that may have plagued your life. It's about cultivating a kind and gentle relationship with yourself, one that counteracts the damaging effects of self-criticism and self-judgment.

For many, self-criticism becomes an unwitting companion, echoing the voices of past rejection. We internalize the negative beliefs others may have held about us, perpetuating a cycle of self-doubt and unworthiness. It's as if we become our own harshest critics, replaying moments of rejection on an endless loop.

Journaling offers a powerful means to unravel this cycle. It provides a safe space to explore the roots of self-criticism and self-judgment to trace them back to their origins. Through self-reflection, you can begin to separate your authentic self from the narrative of rejection.

Furthermore, journaling helps you practice self-compassion. It prompts you to extend to yourself the same empathy and understanding that you would readily offer to a dear friend in times of need. It's about acknowledging your humanity, with all its imperfections, and treating yourself with the love and kindness you deserve.

As you journal and learn to embrace self-compassion, you embark on a journey of self-healing and self-acceptance. You break free from the grip of self-criticism and create a new narrative, one defined by self-worth, resilience, and the understanding that you deserve, both from others and, most importantly, from yourself.

Story Time

Laura had always been the kind of person who put others first. She was incredibly compassionate and caring, always ensuring her friends and family were happy and well cared for. But there was one person she often neglected in this selfless pursuit of taking care of others – herself.

One day, after witnessing her best friend's incredible transformation, Laura had a moment of clarity. Her friend had faced her fears, let go of the past, and started living a life filled with purpose and joy. Laura realized she had allowed her past and insecurities to dictate her future. She had been limiting herself and holding back from pursuing her dreams and desires.

Inspired by her friend's journey, Laura decided it was time to change. She knew she couldn't wait for others to treat her how she deserved to be treated. She needed to become her solution, the source of the love and kindness she had been craving.

Laura embarked on a journey of self-discovery and self-love. She started by forgiving herself for past mistakes and releasing the self-criticism that had held her back for so long. She learned to treat herself with the compassion and kindness she had always shown others.

Each day, Laura made an effort to do something loving for herself. She practiced self-care, set healthy boundaries, and pursued her passions and dreams with renewed vigor. She discovered the joy of saying "yes" to herself and her desires, which was transformative.

Laura noticed a profound shift in her life as she embraced self-love and self-compassion. Her relationships improved, and she attracted people who valued and respected her. She felt more confident and empowered in her choices, and her dreams began to take shape.

Laura had learned that becoming her solution was not a selfish act but a necessary one. By loving and caring for herself, she transformed her own life and inspired others, just as her best friend had been to her. Laura's journey was a testament to the power of self-love and the incredible possibilities that awaited when one decided to become their solution.

Healing and Letting Go

Patience and self-care are crucial to the healing and letting process. It involves nurturing not just your mind but your body and spirit. The journey of healing is gradual, and creating a safe and compassionate space for yourself along the way is crucial.

Patience is vital in this process. Healing from rejection, whether subtle or profound, takes time. Rushing the journey may hinder true transformation. Instead, be patient with yourself, allowing the healing process to unfold at its own pace. Understand that it's okay to have moments of vulnerability, sadness, or anger and that these emotions are part of healing.

Self-care plays a vital role in nurturing your well-being. It's about tending to your physical and emotional needs. Engage in activities that bring you joy, whether in nature, practicing mindfulness, or pursuing creative endeavors. Prioritize self-compassion and self-kindness as you navigate the ups and downs of healing.

Guided journal prompts can be a powerful tool in this process. They provide structure and support for exploring your emotions and experiences. Journaling helps you acknowledge your pain, allowing you to grieve and feel. It's a way to give voice to your innermost thoughts and to make sense of your journey.

Ultimately, you can learn to let go through patience, self-care, and journaling. Letting go doesn't mean forgetting or minimizing the past; instead, it means releasing the grip that past rejection has on your present and future. It's about embracing a lighter heart, an open spirit, and a future filled with hope, self-acceptance, and the capacity to build healthy relationships.

Story Time

Janae had always been the kind of person who cared deeply about others. She had a big heart and a compassionate spirit, but it often came at a cost – her well-being. She found herself in relationships where she was mistreated, belittled, and taken for granted. It was a pattern she had become all too familiar with, and she was tired of it.

One day, as she sat alone in her room, tears streaming down her face, Janae asked herself the tough questions lingering in her mind for years. "Why do I care so much about people who mistreat me? Why do I keep begging them to stay in my life, even when they hurt me? Why do I allow people who belittle me to remain a part of my life?"

As she reflected on these questions, Janae had a moment of clarity. She realized that she had normalized dysfunctional relationships due to her upbringing. Growing up, she had witnessed unhealthy dynamics in her family, which had become a familiar pattern in her adult life.

But in that moment, something shifted within Janae. She had reached a breaking point and decided she couldn't continue down this path of self-neglect and emotional turmoil. She recognized that she deserved better, that her well-being was worth protecting.

Janae chose to stop complaining and waiting for people to leave her life. Instead, she decided to take control of her happiness and set boundaries to protect herself emotionally, physically, and psychologically. It wasn't easy, and there were moments of discomfort and uncertainty, but she was determined to prioritize herself.

Over time, as she implemented her boundaries and distanced herself from toxic relationships, Janae began to feel a profound sense of liberation. She realized that she no longer needed validation or approval from those who had mistreated her. She found strength in self-love and self-respect.

Janae's transformation was not just about setting boundaries but about reclaiming her sense of self-worth. She learned that she could care for others without sacrificing her well-being. It was a powerful lesson that changed the trajectory of her life, and she was finally free from the cycle of dysfunctional relationships.

Cultivating Empowerment

Empowerment is the fruit of your journey – the radiant light that emerges from the shadows of rejection. Step into your power by embracing authenticity, standing up for your beliefs, and pursuing your passions unapologetically. Welcome empowerment to ripple through your life, transforming your relationships, mindset, and overall sense of purpose.

Cultivating empowerment is a transformative journey of self-discovery and self-assertion. It's about recognizing and embracing your inherent worth and capabilities, stepping into your power with confidence and authenticity.

To emerge in your full power, embracing your authenticity is crucial. This means honoring your true self unapologetically and owning your strengths, quirks, and unique qualities. It's about being genuine and unafraid to show up as you are, knowing that your authenticity is your greatest strength.

Empowerment also involves standing up for your beliefs and values. It means having the courage to voice your opinions, even when they may be unpopular or challenging. It's about advocating for what you believe is right and just and being a force for positive change in the world.

Furthermore, empowerment is about pursuing your passions with unwavering dedication. It's about wholeheartedly committing to what brings you joy and purpose and refusing to be held back by fear or external judgments. When you pursue your passions, you tap into a wellspring of energy and enthusiasm that propels you forward.

As you cultivate empowerment, you inspire others, showing them what's possible when one embraces their authentic self, stands up for their beliefs, and pursues their passions with unwavering determination. It's a ripple effect that transforms your own life and can ignite change in the lives of those around you.

Intentional Living

Intentional living is the art of crafting a life that aligns with your values, dreams, and aspirations. Be encouraged to reclaim your narrative and design a life fueled by your passions and desires. You will learn how to detach from the need for external validation and find fulfillment within yourself. Through practical exercises and affirmations, you will embark on a journey of intentional living that celebrates your unique journey.

Embarking on completing this journal is more than just putting pen to paper; it's an act of self-discovery, healing, and transformation. As you delve into the pages of your journal, releasing the weight of past hurt and embracing a mindful approach to your thoughts, you open the door to a profound and prosperous future that awaits you. This transformation isn't merely about changing your circumstances; it's about changing the lens through which you view your life.

Releasing the shackles of past hurt through journaling is a cathartic process. As you put your emotions, experiences, and reflections onto paper, you create a safe space for yourself to confront the pain you've been carrying. By acknowledging these feelings, you permit yourself to heal. Through writing, you begin to untangle the complex web of emotions that have held you captive, allowing them to surface, be acknowledged, and ultimately released.

But the transformation doesn't stop at letting go; it extends into the realm of empowerment and self-discovery. As you shift your focus from dwelling on past hurt to envisioning a prosperous future, you tap into the power of positive intention. Your journal becomes a canvas upon which you paint a vivid picture of the life you aspire to live – a life where you show up for yourself, embrace your worth, and cultivate a deep sense of self-love.

Through mindfulness, you develop an awareness of your thoughts, emotions, and reactions. This mindfulness acts as a guide, helping you navigate the complexities of your inner world with greater clarity. Instead of allowing negative thought patterns to dictate your actions, you become a conscious observer, choosing thoughts that serve your well-being and propel you toward your desired future.

As you engage in this transformative journaling journey, you'll notice subtle shifts in your mindset and outlook. Writing about your prosperous future isn't a mere exercise in wishful thinking; it's a deliberate practice that rewires your brain for positivity. With each affirmation, intention, and visualization, you're reinforcing a new narrative that empowers you, celebrates your uniqueness, and fosters a deep sense of self-belief.

This transformation isn't an overnight process; it's a gradual evolution that unfolds over time. As you consistently journal, release the burden of past hurt, and cultivate mindfulness, you'll find that your relationships with yourself and others begin to shift. You'll notice a newfound sense of empowerment and confidence, affecting every aspect of your life.

Imagine the freedom that comes from releasing the heavy baggage of past hurt. Picture yourself standing tall, unburdened by the weight of resentment, bitterness, and pain. Envision a future where your thoughts are no longer clouded by self-doubt but instead guided by the unwavering belief in your worthiness.

As you complete this journal and transition into a life of mindful thought and empowered action, you are embracing a transformation beyond the pages. You are stepping into the role of the author of your own story, weaving together a narrative that is rooted in healing, growth, and self-love. With each word you write, you are co-creating a future that is prosperous, abundant, and aligned with your most authentic self.

So, as you journey through these pages, remember that you are not only releasing the pain of the past but also setting the stage for a future filled with joy, authenticity, and boundless possibility. The transformation that awaits you is not just a destination but a continuous evolution – a journey of self-discovery that will shape how you perceive yourself, the world around you, and the incredible potential within your grasp.

21 Benefits of a 21-Day Commitment

Cultivating Consistency

Cultivating consistency through a 21-day commitment is critical to reaping the full benefits of journaling. By setting aside time each day, you establish a regular habit that allows you to dive deeper into your thoughts and emotions. This consistency fosters a stronger connection with your inner world, enabling you to track your growth, patterns, and evolving perspectives over time. It's a practice that nurtures self-awareness and personal development, providing a reliable anchor for self-reflection and exploring your unique journey toward healing and growth.

Enhancing Self-Awareness

Enhancing self-awareness through journaling is a powerful process. As you write about your experiences and emotions, you gain valuable insights into your patterns, triggers, and opportunities for personal growth. By exploring your thoughts on paper, you create a space for honest self-reflection, allowing you to understand your reactions and motivations better. This heightened self-awareness becomes a compass, guiding you towards making more informed decisions and fostering healthier relationships, starting with yourself first.

Emotional Healing Journaling

Emotional healing is facilitated through journaling, providing a safe haven to release pent-up emotions. Writing about your feelings offers a cathartic release, allowing you to unburden yourself from the weight of unexpressed emotions. It's a therapeutic process that provides closure to emotional wounds, helping you process and heal from past experiences. Journaling allows you to acknowledge and validate your emotions, ultimately contributing to inner peace and well-being. This emotional healing journey is vital to self-discovery and personal growth, empowering you to navigate life's challenges, including rejections, with greater resilience and authenticity.

Clarity and Focus

Daily reflection through journaling offers a path to clarity and focus. It lets you gain insight into your goals, desires, and challenges. By putting your thoughts on paper, you untangle complex ideas and emotions, paving the way for more informed decision-making and improved problem-solving skills. This clarity becomes a guiding light, helping you navigate the intricate dynamics of overcoming rejections in life with greater purpose and direction. Journaling becomes a transformative tool for honing your vision and maintaining focus on the path to self-discovery and growth.

Mindfulness Journaling

Journaling is a gateway to mindfulness, inviting you to be fully present in the moment. As you put pen to paper, you engage in a process of deep reflection on your experiences and emotions. This introspection encourages you to slow down, observe your thoughts, and be aware of your feelings without judgment. It's a practice that cultivates a sense of mindfulness, helping you stay attuned to the present moment and fostering a greater appreciation for the richness of your inner world. It's a journey that promotes self-awareness, helping you navigate forgiveness with clarity, empathy, and a profound connection to the present moment.

Stress Reduction

Journaling about experiences of rejection can be a powerful stress reduction tool in a private space to express your feelings and concerns without judgment. It provides a safe outlet for processing emotions and finding clarity amid turmoil. As you pour your feelings onto the pages, you release the weight of rejection, gradually alleviating stress. This therapeutic practice contributes to overall well-being, fostering emotional balance in the challenging journey of overcoming rejection. It empowers you to transcend the pain, regain control over your emotions, and ultimately emerge stronger, equipped to navigate life's trials with resilience and grace.

Positive Habit Formation

A 21-day commitment to journaling is not just about writing; it can inspire other positive habits in your daily routine. This practice cultivates discipline, consistency, and self-reflection, setting the stage for personal growth. As you become accustomed to dedicating time each day to journaling, you may find it easier to integrate other habits, such as exercise, meditation, or mindfulness, into your life. This journey of positive habit formation can improve your well-being, empowering you to navigate the complexities of life with greater resilience and intention.

Track Progress

Over 21 days of journaling, you create a tangible journey record. Documenting your thoughts, experiences, and growth provides a rich repository of insights, accomplishments, and progress. This record becomes a valuable resource for self-reflection, allowing you to see how far you've come and evolved. It's a testament to your commitment to personal development and self-discovery. Tracking your progress through journaling fosters a sense of achievement and reminds you of the resilience and growth you're capable of. This documented journey empowers you to navigate the intricate dynamics of life with greater confidence and clarity.

Boosting Self-Esteem

Celebrating achievements and moments of joy through journaling can significantly boost self-esteem and contribute to a more positive self-image. By recording your successes, big and small, you acknowledge your accomplishments and affirm your worth. This practice helps shift your focus away from self-doubt and reinforces a belief in your capabilities. As you revisit these positive moments in your journal, you create a foundation of self-assurance and confidence.

Empowerment

Consistent journaling is a powerful pathway to empowerment. As you engage in daily reflection and self-expression, you gain a heightened control over your thoughts, emotions, and actions. This practice encourages active self-awareness and self-compassion, enabling you to confront challenges with greater resilience and understanding. By documenting your journey, you become the author of your narrative, fostering a deep sense of empowerment. This newfound strength guides you to face obstacles confidently and proactively work on your inner strength, ultimately shaping a more fulfilling and authentic path forward.

Write Freely

Approach journaling with an open mind and a sense of freedom. Release the burden of worrying about grammar or structure; let your thoughts flow freely onto the page. This practice is about self-expression and self-discovery, not perfection. Embrace the spontaneity of your thoughts and emotions as they arise. Allowing your writing to be unfiltered and unguarded creates a space for honesty and authenticity. Your journal becomes a trusted confidant, ready to receive your innermost musings without judgment. This liberated form of writing is a gateway to self-reflection, emotional release, and personal growth within the context of releasing your attachment to the thoughts, approval, opinions, and words of others.

Embrace Honesty

Embrace honesty in your journaling practice. Authenticity is the cornerstone of self-discovery and personal growth. Being genuine and open in your writing unlocks more profound layers of self-awareness. This raw and unfiltered expression allows you to explore your thoughts, emotions, and experiences without reservation. It's a space to confront challenges, celebrate victories, and love and appreciate yourself wholeheartedly. Embracing honesty in your journaling journey empowers you to cultivate a more genuine connection with yourself and those around you. It's a transformative practice leading to greater self-acceptance and a richer understanding of your journey.

Reflect on Your Day

Reflecting on your day through journaling is a valuable practice. Use your journal as a canvas to explore your experiences, emotions, and interactions. Ask yourself what brought you joy and what challenged you. Dive into your thoughts and feelings, unearthing valuable insights and revelations. This daily reflection allows you to process your experiences and better understand yourself. It's a pathway to self-awareness, resilience, and personal growth beyond the noise and opinions of others. Through this practice, you navigate the intricacies of your journey with greater clarity and authenticity.

Explore Feelings

Explore your feelings through journaling, delving into the spectrum of positive and negative emotions. Give voice to your inner world on paper. Expressing your feelings creates a safe, non-judgmental space to process and understand them better. This practice allows you to gain insight into the root causes of your emotions, triggers, and response patterns. It fosters emotional intelligence, self-awareness, and resilience. Embracing your feelings, even the challenging ones, is a transformative step toward healing and creating the life you love.

Celebrate Achievements

Celebrate your achievements, no matter how small, through journaling. Acknowledging your accomplishments is a powerful practice that cultivates a sense of pride and motivation. You validate your efforts and progress by recording these successes in your journal. This positive reinforcement boosts your self-esteem and encourages you to strive for your goals. Recognizing your achievements becomes a source of empowerment, reminding you of your capabilities and resilience toward a more fulfilling and authentic life.

Set Intentions

Utilize journaling to set intentions for your day or to visualize your long-term goals. The act of writing these intentions down enhances your commitment to achieving them. Whether outlining your daily priorities or envisioning your aspirations, putting your choices on paper makes them more tangible and concrete. It's a powerful tool for staying focused and motivated. Journaling becomes the compass guiding you toward your desired destinations, helping you maintain clarity and purpose in your journey of self-discovery and growth.

Release Stress

Release stress and worries onto the pages of your journal. This practice offers a therapeutic outlet for the burdens you may carry. You create a sense of relief and clarity by expressing your concerns. Your journal becomes a trusted confidant, ready to receive your thoughts and emotions without judgment. This process helps you untangle the complexity of your stressors, allowing you to gain perspective and a deeper understanding of your challenges. Journaling offers a safe space for emotional release, contributing to your overall well-being as you navigate life's intricacies, providing a sense of catharsis and emotional balance.

Boundaries

Journaling is a powerful tool for setting and reinforcing boundaries. Start by reflecting on the areas where you feel your limits are tested or violated, whether in your role as a loved one, friend, lover, or colleague. Write down your thoughts and emotions surrounding these situations. This process helps you clarify your limits and why they are essential.

Next, use your journal to plan how you will communicate your boundaries assertively and respectfully. Write out scripts or strategies for addressing boundary issues. Journaling allows you to rehearse and refine your approach, making setting and maintaining boundaries in real-life situations easier.

As you journal, you can explore any underlying beliefs or fears holding you back from setting boundaries. Uncovering and addressing these internal barriers can strengthen your resolve to establish healthy limits and protect your well-being. Journaling is a valuable companion in your journey toward effective boundary-setting and self-care.

Inner Peace

Journaling is a potent tool to restore inner peace amid life's complexities. Begin by expressing your thoughts and emotions without judgment. This cathartic release helps you process inner turmoil. Identify stressors and their triggers, mapping out strategies for addressing them.

Use your journal to create a daily gratitude list, focusing on positive aspects of your life. This practice cultivates optimism and reduces anxiety. Reflect on your values and goals, aligning your actions with what truly matters. Journaling offers a sacred space for self-compassion, nurturing emotional well-being, and fostering inner peace, empowering you to navigate life with grace and tranquility.

Self-Forgiveness

Embracing self-forgiveness through journaling is a transformative journey. Begin by acknowledging past mistakes and self-criticism without judgment. Write about the emotions tied to these experiences, allowing yourself to feel and express them.

Journaling provides a safe space to explore the lessons learned from your actions. Reflect on how those experiences have shaped you and your growth.

Write self-forgiveness letters to yourself, offering understanding and compassion.

As you continue this practice, you'll gradually release the burden of guilt and self-blame. Journaling becomes a path to self-acceptance, healing, and, ultimately, the liberation of your heart and soul. It empowers you to forgive yourself, nurturing inner peace and self-compassion during your life's journey.

Clear Communication

Journaling is a potent tool for enhancing communication skills. Write down your thoughts, emotions, and reflections on past conversations or conflicts. Analyze your communication patterns, identifying areas for improvement.

Practice writing out what you want to say before engaging in difficult conversations. This helps you clarify your message and intentions. Journaling also offers a space to vent frustrations or emotions privately, reducing the chances of emotional outbursts during conversations.

Moreover, use your journal to reflect on your active listening skills, noting moments when you genuinely understood others and areas where you could improve. By journaling consistently, you foster self-awareness and refine your communication abilities, enhancing your effectiveness in redefining your relationships.

In 21 days, journaling becomes more than a practice – a source of empowerment, self-awareness, and growth. As you put pen to paper, you embark on a journey of understanding, healing, and celebration that has the potential to positively transform your relationship with yourself and the world around you.

Embracing the Journey

As you embark on this transformative journey of forgiveness, healing, and empowerment, remember that you are the author of your story. Your experiences, emotions, and choices are the brushstrokes that paint the canvas of your life. Within these pages, you will find the guidance, support, and inspiration to navigate the complexities of rejection and emerge on the other side with a lighter heart, a freer spirit, and a sense of self that is unapologetically radiant.

So, pick up your pen and let it dance across the pages. Let the ink weave a tapestry of healing and empowerment—an intimate conversation with yourself that leads to renewal. Embrace the transformative power of journaling and step into a future where you stand tall, unburdened by the weight of wounds, and radiate with the radiance of self-love and the beauty of your unique journey.

I Forgive My Mind For Believing My Parents Rejected Me

Forgiveness Inner Reflection of the Day

As I embark on this journey of forgiveness, I turn my gaze inward and reflect on the intricate workings of my mind. I recognize that my mind has woven a web of beliefs based on my unmet expectations from my parents. I choose to forgive my mind for carrying the burden of feeling rejected and unloved for attaching these feelings to the actions of my parents.

In its quest to make sense of the world, my mind has formed interpretations that might not accurately reflect reality. I release the grip of these beliefs and offer compassion for relying on them to understand my experiences, limitations, and life circumstances. I dismiss the notion that their actions were solely intended to reject me. I let go of the heavy burden of resentment that I've carried due to these unmet expectations.

Instead of holding onto these beliefs, I invite curiosity and openness. I replace judgment with understanding, seeking to uncover the complexities behind their actions. I recognize that forgiving my mind for clinging to these limiting beliefs is essential to my healing and growth.

As I release the grip of these thoughts, I make space for new perspectives and the possibility of healing. My parents' actions do not define my worth or lovability. I am ready to reclaim my power and create a new narrative—one that is centered on self-love, acceptance, and understanding.

In forgiving my mind for perpetuating these beliefs, I pave the way for a transformative journey toward healing. I commit to nurturing a more compassionate relationship with myself, which enables me to release the shackles of resentment and embrace a more liberated and empowered sense of self.

Meditative Thought of the Day

In the gentle embrace of self-compassion, I release the weight of unmet expectations set by my parents. I recognize that their hopes and dreams, while well-intentioned, were not meant to define my path. With every breath, I let go of the need to live up to their desires, allowing myself to step into my authentic journey.

As I release these expectations, I free myself from the burden of seeking external approval. I reclaim my power to define success and fulfillment on my terms. Each moment of self-forgiveness allows me to nurture my aspirations and dreams without the shadows of should-haves.

In the space of acceptance, I find liberation from the chains of comparison and judgment. I honor the unique path that I've forged, acknowledging that my worth is not determined by meeting someone else's ideals. With gratitude for the lessons learned, I step forward with a heart unburdened by the weight of unmet expectations.

I am the author of my narrative, and in this release, I embrace the beauty of my journey as it unfolds. With kindness towards myself, I let go of the need to seek validation from unattainable standards. I find solace in the love and acceptance that I cultivate within, knowing that my worth is inherent and not bound by the expectations of others.

Deeper Connection Within

1. What is the origin of my fear of rejection, and how can I rewrite this narrative?

_____

_____

_____

_____

_____

2. How have past rejections shaped my present mindset, and how can I reframe them positively?

_____

_____

_____

_____

_____

3. What strengths and qualities do I possess that make me resilient in the face of rejection?

_____

_____

_____

_____

_____

Loving Statements About Me

I am capable of achieving greatness in every aspect of my life.

My potential is limitless, and I am worthy of success and happiness.

I believe in my abilities and trust the journey I am on.

Gratitude Reflection of the Day

I'm grateful for the wisdom I've blessed me with, allowing me to see my worth and celebrate myself in every chapter of life. I am thankful for the lessons learned from my past, and I trust myself in the future.

Inner Reflections

I Forgive My Mind For Believing My Family Rejects And Belittles My Creative Ideas

Forgiveness Inner Reflection of the Day

In this moment of introspection, I turn my attention to the internal landscape of my mind. My thoughts have been shaped by the belief that my family rejects and belittles my creative ideas. I choose to embark on a journey of forgiveness, starting with forgiving my mind for allowing these beliefs to take root.

My mind has been a fertile ground for doubts and insecurities, often stemming from past experiences. I release the grip of these beliefs and forgive myself for allowing them to influence my self-worth and creative expression.

My family's reactions may have been colored by their perspectives, experiences, and biases. I let go of the heavy weight of resentment and desire to offer myself the gift of self-compassion. My creativity is a unique and valuable part of my identity.

As I forgive my mind for clinging to these limiting beliefs, I open myself up to new possibilities. I choose to replace self-doubt with self-assurance, replacing fear with curiosity. I release the need for external validation and embrace the power of self-belief.

By forgiving my mind, I release the shackles that have held me back from fully expressing myself. I am no longer bound by the past or by others' perceptions. I am free to explore, create, and innovate without the burden of judgment.

I commit to nurturing a more supportive and empowering inner dialogue. I believe in the worthiness of my creative ideas, regardless of others' reactions. Forgiving my mind is crucial to reclaiming my confidence and owning my creative voice.

In this journey of forgiveness, I embrace the opportunity to heal and grow. I release the old patterns of self-doubt and embrace the boundless potential of my creativity. With each forgiving thought, I step closer to a brighter and more authentic expression of myself.

I forgive my mind for believing my family rejects and belittles my creative ideas.

Meditative Healing Thought of the Day

In the sanctuary of my being, I free myself from the chains of others' opinions. I embrace the boundless strength within, nurturing the flame of self-assuredness. With every breath, I release the grip of external judgments and step into the radiant light of my truth.

I am the architect of my destiny, and I choose to listen to the wisdom of my heart rather than the world's noise. I honor my uniqueness, unburdened by the need for validation. In this sacred space, I find liberation from the weight of approval-seeking.

With each moment of self-acceptance, I weave a tapestry of self-love that shields me from the criticisms of others. I stand tall, rooted in the unshakable knowing of my worth. As I embrace my authentic self, I blossom into a beacon of authenticity, unafraid to shine brightly.

In the tender embrace of self-compassion, I reclaim my power and let the whispers of doubt fade away. The opinions of others hold no sway over my journey, for I walk the path that resonates with my soul. With grace and courage, I release the need for external validation and embrace the freedom to be wholly and unapologetically myself.

Deeper Connection Within

1. How can I focus on those who support and uplift me instead of dwelling on those who reject me?

_____

_____

_____

_____

_____

2. What steps can I take to build a strong foundation of self-worth and self-love?

_____

_____

_____

_____

_____

3. How does rejection from others reflect their insecurities and biases rather than my true worth?

_____

_____

_____

_____

_____

Loving Statements About Me

I am resilient and can overcome any challenges that come my way.

I am deserving of all the positive outcomes and opportunities that life presents.

I embrace change and see it as a chance to evolve and improve.

Gratitude Reflection of the Day

I am thankful for the boldness to embrace my uniqueness and the confidence to let go of self-doubt. I will celebrate my strengths and acknowledge my growth, knowing that love guides me through every step.

Inner Reflections

I Forgive My Mind For Believing My Friends Reject & Minimize My Business

Forgiveness Inner Reflection of the Day

In this moment of deep reflection, I turn my gaze inward to the realm of my thoughts and emotions. I acknowledge that my mind has been carrying the weight of the belief that my friends reject and minimize my business endeavors. With a compassionate heart, I choose to embark on a journey of self-forgiveness.

Like a canvas, I recognize that my mind has been painted with doubts and fears based on past experiences. I release these negative thoughts and offer forgiveness for allowing them to shape my perception of my friends and businesses. Their perspectives, experiences, and circumstances might influence my friends' reactions. As I forgive my mind for clinging to these beliefs, I also release any resentment I may have held towards them.

In this act of self-forgiveness, I free myself from the burden of carrying the weight of perceived rejection. I let go of the need for external validation and instead focused on nurturing self-belief and confidence.

I commit to cultivating a positive and empowering inner dialogue. I recognize that I am creating space for new and affirming beliefs to take root by forgiving my mind. I view my business endeavors through a lens of self-assurance and resilience.

As I release the grip of these limiting thoughts, I also release their hold on my potential. I embrace the power of forgiveness to heal old wounds and create a pathway for growth.

I choose to believe in the value of my business, regardless of others' opinions. By forgiving my mind, I invite a sense of liberation and clarity. With each step of this forgiveness journey, I enter a space of authenticity where my business reflects my passion and purpose.

In forgiveness, I find healing. As I release my mind from the shackles of self-doubt, I open myself to a world of possibilities. With every forgiving thought, I am reclaiming my confidence, reshaping my beliefs, and paving the way for success and fulfillment in my business journey.

I forgive my mind for believing my friends reject me and minimize my business.

Meditative Healing Thought of the Day

In the garden of my soul, I tend to the blossoms of belief and cast away the weeds of rejection. I shift my focus from the shadows of those who turn away to the radiant sunbeams of those who stand by my side. Their unwavering faith nourishes my spirit.

With each step I take, I honor the ones who see my worth and encourage my growth. Their presence is a testament to the beauty I bring into their lives, a reminder that my light is cherished and valued. In their embrace, I find solace and strength.

I release the weight of others' opinions that no longer serve me, allowing them to flutter away like autumn leaves in the wind. Instead, I embrace the warmth of encouragement and appreciation surrounding me. Their belief becomes the armor that shields me from doubt and negativity.

As I journey forward, I am guided by the love and support of those beside me. Their faith becomes a beacon, illuminating the path of my purpose. With gratitude, I leave behind the echoes of rejection and welcome the symphony of affirmation and love that resonates within and around me.

Deeper Connection Within

1. What affirmations can I repeat to myself daily to reinforce my self-confidence and worthiness?

_____

_____

_____

_____

_____

2. How can I turn rejection into a source of motivation to prove my potential to myself?

_____

_____

_____

_____

_____

3. What activities or hobbies bring joy and help me reconnect with my true self?

_____

_____

_____

_____

_____

Loving Statements About Me

I am confident in my unique talents and the value I bring to the world.

I trust my intuition to guide me towards the right decisions and choices.

I am constantly growing and expanding my knowledge and skills.

Gratitude Reflection of the Day

I am thankful for the happiness in my life. Regardless of circumstances, I find joy in every moment, and my heart overflows with gratitude for grace, inner peace, and kind thoughts about myself.

Inner Reflections

DAY 4

I Forgive The Rejection And Judgment In Religious Spaces

Forgiveness Inner Reflection of the Day

In the depths of my inner reflection, I confront the shadows of past experiences where I felt rejected and judged within religious spaces. I recognize these memories' weight and impact on my emotional well-being.

With an open heart, I choose to embark on a journey of forgiveness. I extend compassion to myself for carrying the burden of these painful experiences. The actions of others may have been rooted in their perspectives and beliefs rather than a reflection of my worth.

In this moment of self-forgiveness, I release the grip of resentment and hurt that has been holding me back. I choose to let go of the attachment to the judgment and rejection I have encountered. As I do so, I create space for healing and growth within my heart.

I recognize that forgiveness is not about condoning hurtful actions but about liberating myself from their hold. By forgiving, I choose to free myself from the weight of negativity within me.

In forgiving these experiences, I am reclaiming my power and self-worth. I am choosing to move forward with a heart unburdened by the pain of the past. I am again opening myself to the possibility of finding connection and acceptance within religious spaces.

As I release these old wounds, I also remove the limitations they have placed on my spiritual journey. I choose to cultivate a sense of inner peace and self-compassion. I am no longer defined by the rejection and judgment I have faced but by my capacity to heal and forgive.

In forgiveness, I can transcend the past and embrace a brighter future. I am choosing to create my spiritual path, one that is guided by love, understanding, and acceptance. As I forgive, I let go of what no longer serves me and step into a spiritual liberation and growth space.

I forgive the rejection and judgment felt in any religious space.

Meditative Healing Thought of the Day

In the sanctuary of my soul, I find liberation from the confines of judgment and expectations. I embrace my spirituality with an open heart, transcending the limitations that others may impose. Their perceptions do not define my connection to the divine.

I release the weight of dogma and embrace the expansiveness of my own beliefs. My spiritual journey is a unique tapestry woven with threads of my experiences and revelations. I can explore, question, and grow on my terms.

As I stand firm in my authenticity, I allow my light to shine, undiminished by the opinions of others. I cultivate a sacred space where love, acceptance, and connection with the divine flourish. I am empowered to live my truth, unburdened by the constraints of religious norms.

In this sacred dance of self-discovery, I honor the whispers of my soul and the universe's guidance. I am a vessel of divine energy, radiating love and compassion. I walk this path with grace, confident that my spirituality is a reflection of my unique essence. In this realization, I find true bliss beyond religious limitations.

Deeper Connection Within

1. How can I embrace rejection as a pathway to growth and learning?

_____
_____
_____
_____
_____

2. How can I practice self-compassion and treat myself with the same kindness I offer others?

_____
_____
_____
_____
_____

3. What limiting beliefs about rejection, do I need to challenge and replace with empowering beliefs?

_____
_____
_____
_____
_____

Loving Statements About Me

I am open to receiving abundance and creating a life I love.

I release self-doubt and replace it with self-assurance and positivity.

I am a magnet for success, which naturally flows into my life.

Gratitude Reflection of the Day

In my journey through life, I am thankful for the courage to accept my past without letting it define me and by releasing regrets and mistakes, knowing that forgiveness and love empower me to move forward.

Inner Reflections

I Forgive Any Rejection From People Who Left Me Emotionally Bruised

Forgiveness Inner Reflection of the Day

In the depths of my inner reflection, I confront the pain of rejection from those who have left me emotionally bruised. I acknowledge the wounds these experiences have inflicted upon my heart and spirit, and I choose to embark on a journey of forgiveness.

As I gaze into the recesses of my soul, I recognize forgiveness's power. It is not about absolving others of their actions but about releasing myself from the grip of resentment and hurt. I choose to release the heavy burden of carrying these wounds and the weight of their impact on my self-esteem.

In forgiving those who have rejected me, I am granting myself the gift of freedom. I acknowledge that their actions may have stemmed from their pain, insecurities, or misunderstandings. I let go of the negative emotions that have held me captive and make space for healing and growth.

As I extend forgiveness, I also extend compassion to myself and those who have hurt me. I recognize that I deserve love and acceptance, regardless of others' actions. By forgiving, I release the power these experiences have held over me and regain control of my emotions and self-worth.

Forgiveness is a declaration of my strength and resilience. It signifies my commitment to my own well-being and inner peace. By letting go of the hurt, I create room for positivity and growth to flourish within me.

As I journey toward forgiveness, I no longer define myself by the rejection that has wounded me. I am choosing to rise above the pain and embrace the possibility of a brighter, more empowered future. By forgiving, I am taking steps toward healing, allowing my heart to mend, and paving the way for greater self-love and acceptance.

In forgiveness, I find liberation—a release from the chains of hurt and a pathway to inner harmony. I choose to move forward with an unburdened heart, a resilient spirit, and a soul open to the possibilities that await.

People may experience rejection in friendships when they feel excluded, ignored, or no longer included in their social circle. This can be particularly hurtful when it involves the loss of a close friend or when friends intentionally distance themselves.

Meditative Healing Thought of the Day

In the gentle embrace of self-love, I tend to the wounds that time may have left behind. I acknowledge the emotional bruises and offer them the soothing balm of compassion. Each bruise is a testament to my strength; I have endured and grown.

With each breath, I release the weight of past pain, allowing it to dissipate like morning mist. I choose to heal, not by denying the bruises, but by allowing myself to feel and then to let go. I am not defined by the hurt but by the resilience that mends the broken places.

As I offer forgiveness to myself and those who may have caused the bruises, I open the door to transformation. I reclaim my power by choosing healing over lingering pain. The remaining scars remind me of my journey and ability to transcend adversity.

In this sacred healing space, I reclaim my emotional well-being and nurture the garden of my heart. I allow the light of self-love to touch even the deepest wounds, turning them into sources of wisdom and compassion. With each step forward, I am guided by the knowledge that I am healing, and in healing, I am reclaiming my joy and peace.

Deeper Connection Within

1. How can I use my experiences of rejection to empathize and connect with others who have faced similar challenges?

_____

_____

_____

_____

_____

2. What unique qualities make me stand out, and how can I celebrate them?

_____

_____

_____

_____

_____

3. How can I shift my focus from seeking external validation to cultivating self-validation?

_____

_____

_____

_____

_____

Loving Statements About Me

I am in control of my thoughts, and I choose to focus on the positive.

I deserve love, respect, and all the good things life offers.

I acknowledge my achievements and celebrate my progress.

Gratitude Reflection of the Day

I am thankful for unwavering confidence in who I am—recognizing my value and refusing to compare myself to others.

Inner Reflections

I Forgive Co-Workers For Rejecting My Kindness And Gossiping Behind My Back

Forgiveness Inner Reflection of the Day

In the stillness of my introspection, I confront the sting of rejection from co-workers who have misunderstood my intentions and gossiped behind me. I choose to embark on a path of forgiveness—a journey that liberates me from the weight of negativity and resentment.

As I delve into my emotions, I recognize that forgiveness is a gift I offer to myself rather than an endorsement of hurtful actions. I release the grip of anger and disappointment, allowing space for healing and growth within my heart.

Forgiveness is an act of courage—an assertion of my inner strength. Acknowledging that people's reactions may be shaped by their experiences and insecurities. By forgiving, I'm not excusing their behavior but releasing its power over me.

In extending forgiveness, I also extend compassion to myself and those who have hurt me. I let go of the narrative that paints me as a victim and instead empower myself to understand that others' opinions do not determine my worth.

Choosing forgiveness doesn't negate the pain I've felt, but it allows me to reclaim my emotional well-being. I release the hold of negative energy clouding my interactions and replace it with a renewed sense of inner peace.

Through forgiveness, I create a pathway toward positive change. I choose to rise above the gossip and rejection, focusing on fostering a healthy work environment and meaningful relationships. By letting go of grudges, I open myself to the potential of building bridges and deepening connections.

As I journey through forgiveness, I'm not erasing the past but rewriting my future. I'm investing in my growth, learning, and personal development. By forgiving, I step into the light of self-empowerment and resilience, paving the way for a brighter, more harmonious work life.

In forgiveness, I find liberation from the grip of negativity. I release the weight of resentment and embrace the freedom to move forward with an unburdened heart, a renewed spirit, and a resolve to create a workplace built on understanding, empathy, and mutual respect.

Meditative Healing Thought of the Day

Amidst the whispers of others, I find solace in my truth. I restore my kindness and grace, undeterred by the gossip that swirls around me. The opinions of others do not define me; I am the curator of my character.

With each step, I erect boundaries safeguarding my authenticity and well-being. I recognize that setting boundaries is an act of self-respect, an affirmation of my worthiness. The echoes of gossip are mere ripples in the vast ocean of my existence.

Restoring my kindness and establishing boundaries, I free myself from the weight of external judgment. My actions reflect my values and intentions, unaffected by the whispers of those who do not honestly know my heart. I stand firm in my authenticity, embracing my journey with unwavering self-assurance.

I release the need for external validation in the gentle glow of self-empowerment. I find strength in my choices and resilience in my resolve. The shadows of gossip may linger, but I walk in the light of my truth, knowing that my kindness and boundaries are my gifts to myself, undiminished by the opinions of others.

Deeper Connection Within

1. How can I set healthy boundaries that protect my emotional well-being?

_____

_____

_____

_____

_____

2. How can I visualize a future where I thrive despite rejection, embracing my full potential?

_____

_____

_____

_____

_____

3. How does rejection serve as a filter that guides me toward the people and opportunities aligned with my journey?

_____

_____

_____

_____

_____

Loving Statements About Me

My past does not define me; my future empowers me.

I radiate confidence and inspire others with my self-belief.

I am a unique individual with a purpose that only I can fulfill.

Gratitude Reflection of the Day

I am grateful for the strength to overcome challenges. I am resilient and capable of rising above difficulties and finding solace in knowing I have everything within me to thrive and achieve greatness.

Inner Reflections

I Forgive My Peers For Rejecting Me By Constantly Judging My Success

Forgiveness Inner Reflection of the Day

In the depths of my soul-searching, I confront the feelings of hurt and inadequacy caused by my peers' constant judgment and rejection regarding my successes. I embark on a journey of forgiveness—a transformative path that frees me from the shackles of external validation.

As I delve into my emotions, I realize that forgiveness is an act of self-empowerment. It is not an endorsement of others' opinions but a conscious choice to release their hold on my self-worth. I acknowledge that people's judgments often stem from insecurities and unmet aspirations.

Forgiveness is an internal shift, a decision to liberate myself from the burden of seeking approval. It's about dismantling the walls of comparison and embracing my unique path. By forgiving, I focus on my journey rather than allowing external judgments to dictate my worth.

Through forgiveness, I find solace in my accomplishments. I choose to release the grip of negativity and criticism, recognizing that others' perceptions of my success do not determine my value. By forgiving, I prefer to validate myself and celebrate my achievements wholeheartedly.

In extending forgiveness, I extend compassion to myself and my peers. I release the cycle of resentment and replace it with understanding. I recognize that everyone is on their path, navigating their struggles and victories. By forgiving, I liberate myself from the burden of holding onto grudges.

Choosing forgiveness doesn't erase the pain of rejection, but it allows me to heal and move forward with strength. I let go of the need for external validation and embrace the power of self-acceptance. Through forgiveness, I rekindle my self-confidence and pave the way for a brighter, more authentic future.

In forgiveness, I uncover the key to my happiness and growth. I release the weight of judgment and rejection, allowing space for self-love and self-compassion to flourish. By forgiving, I step into a realm of self-assuredness and resilience, fostering a deep connection with my true self and inviting positivity into every aspect of my life.

I forgive my peers for rejecting me by constantly judging my success.

Meditative Healing Thought of the Day

In the tapestry of my life, I paint my success with strokes of determination and passion. As I rise above the judgment of others, I realize that their perceptions do not define my worth. My success is a testament to my dedication and potential, shining bright despite the shadows of skepticism.

I embrace the power of self-belief, understanding that my journey is uniquely mine to navigate. Like passing clouds, others' opinions hold no dominion over my path. I walk forward with confidence, unburdened by the weight of their judgment.

With each achievement, I find liberation from the need for external validation. The doubts or criticisms of others do not diminish my success; it is my triumph, a celebration of my capabilities and resilience.

I stand tall in the realm of my achievements, knowing that my potential knows no bounds. The judgment of others is a fleeting echo in the vast landscape of my accomplishments. I am the author of my narrative, and I choose to fill its pages with unwavering self-assurance and the vibrant hues of my success.

Deeper Connection Within

1. How can I practice mindfulness to stay present and avoid getting caught up in negative thoughts about rejection?

_____

_____

_____

_____

_____

2. What supportive communities, mentors, or resources can I seek to surround myself with positivity?

_____

_____

_____

_____

_____

3. How can I reframe rejection as redirection, leading me to opportunities that are better suited for me?

_____

_____

_____

_____

_____

Loving Statements About Me

I let go of comparison and embrace my journey with grace.

I am resilient in the face of adversity and always find a way to rise.

I am deserving of self-care and make my well-being a priority.

Gratitude Reflection of the Day

I celebrate my achievements, big and small, with a heart full of gratitude. I see each accomplishment as a testament to my persistence and my determination.

Inner Reflections

I Forgive Society For Rejecting Me Due to Their Unrealistic Expectations

Forgiveness Inner Reflection of the Day

In the sanctuary of introspection, I confront the scars of society's rejection driven by unrealistic expectations. I embark on a journey of forgiveness, liberating myself from the weight of societal demands and rediscovering my authentic self.

Forgiving society is a revolutionary act of self-love and empowerment. It acknowledges that societal norms are often crafted from the opinions of many, which can never truly encapsulate the depth of my being. By forgiving, I free myself from the pressure of fitting into a mold never designed for me.

Forgiveness is not an endorsement of societal standards but a reclamation of my worth. It's about breaking the chains of conformity and embracing my uniqueness. By forgiving, I honor my individuality and prioritize my well-being over society's expectations.

Through forgiveness, I find strength in vulnerability. I realize that societal pressures can stem from their struggles and insecurities. By forgiving, I choose empathy over resentment, understanding that everyone is navigating their battles.

Forgiveness is the gateway to authenticity. It enables me to release the shame and insecurity that society's rejection has imposed upon me. By forgiving, I unburden myself from the false narratives of inadequacy and recognize my inherent value beyond societal judgments.

In extending forgiveness, I embrace self-compassion. I recognize that I deserve love and acceptance, regardless of whether society acknowledges it. By forgiving, I create space to nurture a positive relationship with myself, grounded in self-worth.

Choosing to forgive society does not mean erasing the pain but transforming it into strength. In forgiveness, I reclaim my power and reshape my narrative. I release the grip of societal expectations and step into the light of self-acceptance. It's about rewriting the narrative and defining my path, unencumbered by societal dictates. By forgiving, I embark on self-discovery and redefine success on my terms.

Being intentionally left out or excluded from social activities, gatherings, or group settings can be a form of rejection. This can happen among friends, peers, or workplace or community environments.

Meditative Healing Thought of the Day

I embrace the gentle wisdom of setting realistic expectations creating a foundation for fulfillment and growth. Like seeds sown in fertile soil, I nurture goals that align with my abilities and circumstances. Through this balance, I cultivate a garden of achievement that flourishes.

I release the burden of chasing perfection and instead find contentment in progress. With each step forward, I acknowledge that success is not always linear, and setbacks are stepping stones to understanding. By setting attainable milestones, I build a staircase of accomplishments, each step a testament to my resilience.

I view challenges as opportunities for growth, embracing the lessons they bring. Realistic expectations allow space for unforeseen circumstances, reminding me that life's journey combines victories and lessons. As I align my aspirations with reality, I release the weight of disappointment and embrace the freedom of achievable goals.

With a heart open to learning and a mind attuned to reality, I navigate the currents of life with grace. I celebrate each milestone, no matter how small, knowing that progress is the beacon guiding me forward. In setting realistic expectations, I create a foundation of empowerment and self-compassion that leads me to a place of true success.

Deeper Connection Within

1. What qualities and experiences can I focus on to build confident self-esteem?

_____

_____

_____

_____

_____

2. How can I channel my energy into creative pursuits that bring me joy and fulfillment?

_____

_____

_____

_____

_____

3. How can I find gratitude in the face of rejection, appreciating the lessons and growth it brings?

_____

_____

_____

_____

_____

Loving Statements About Me

I attract positive energy and positive outcomes into my life.

I trust that all things are conspiring in my favor.

I am fearless in pursuing my dreams and taking calculated risks.

Gratitude Reflection of the Day

I am thankful for letting go of negative self-perceptions. I find confidence in the unique qualities within me.

Inner Reflections

DAY 9

I Forgive My Mind For Judging People Who Decline My Services And Internalizing It As A Rejection

Forgiveness Inner Reflection of the Day

Within the chambers of self-reflection, I confront the shadow of my judgments, which label perceived rejection as a reflection of my self-worth. Through the healing grace of forgiveness, I embrace a journey towards inner liberation and self-acceptance.

Forgiving my mind for its tendency to judge is an act of compassion towards myself. I acknowledge that judgments stem from my insecurities and need for external validation. By extending forgiveness, I grant myself the space to release the weight of self-criticism.

Forgiveness is not a validation of my mind's judgments but a declaration of my commitment to inner peace. It's a conscious choice to untangle myself from the webs of negativity that judgments weave. By forgiving, I free myself from the shackles of self-doubt and self-critique.

Through forgiveness, I tap into the wellspring of empathy. I recognize that factors beyond my control often influence people's decisions. By forgiving, I shift my focus from internalizing perceived rejections to understanding the complexities of human choices.

Forgiveness is an invitation to relinquish the armor of defensiveness. It enables me to see beyond my ego and embrace a broader perspective. By forgiving, I foster connections rooted in understanding rather than reacting from a place of hurt.

In extending forgiveness, I nurture self-compassion. I acknowledge that external responses do not define my worth. By forgiving, I redirect my energy towards self-care and self-love, regardless of others' decisions.

Choosing to forgive my mind's judgments is an affirmation of my self-worth. It's about redefining my narrative and recognizing that my value remains intact, irrespective of others' choices. By forgiving, I shift my focus from external validation to an internal wellspring of confidence.

In forgiveness, I offer myself the gift of healing. I release the grip of my mind's judgments and open my heart to a newfound sense of peace. By forgiving, I create a fertile ground for self-growth and empowerment, where the foundation of my self-worth remains unshaken by the ebb and flow of external circumstances.

Artists, writers, and creators may face rejection when publishers, galleries, or critics reject their work. This can be discouraging, as it challenges their artistic abilities and aspirations.

I forgive my mind for judging people who decline my services and internalizing it as a rejection.

Meditative Healing Thought of the Day

I free myself from the chains of internalized rejection, recognizing that the opinions of others are not a reflection of my worth. Like a rock standing firm amidst the waves, I anchor my self-esteem in the depths of self-love. I release the grip of seeking external validation and honor my worth.

Each rejection is a fleeting moment in the grand tapestry of life, a tiny brushstroke in the canvas of my journey. I refuse to paint my self-worth with the colors of others' perceptions. Instead, I wield the brush of self-acceptance, coloring my life with the hues of resilience and confidence.

I nourish my soul with affirmations of self-love, letting go of the weight of past rejections. As I embrace my unique essence, I transcend the need for approval, basking in the light of my authenticity. I am not defined by rejection but by my strength to rise above it.

With each breath, I inhale the power to reclaim my self-worth and exhale the doubt that has held me back. I stand tall in my truth, allowing the winds of criticism to pass, leaving me unshaken. I am worthy, whole, and deserving of love and acceptance from within and the world around me.

Deeper Connection Within

1. What self-care practices can I implement to nurture my emotional and mental well-being?

_____

_____

_____

_____

_____

2. How can I recognize rejection as a part of life's journey and not a reflection of my worth?

_____

_____

_____

_____

3. What steps can I take to release the burden of seeking approval from others?

_____

_____

_____

_____

Loving Statements About Me

I am grateful for the opportunities that come my way, big or small.

I release any limiting beliefs that have held me back from my potential.

I am the author of my own success story and create my reality.

Gratitude Reflection of the Day

I am thankful for the healing power of self-acceptance. I am grateful for the ability to forgive myself for past mistakes and embrace the person I am today, knowing that my love is enough.

Inner Reflections

I Forgive Myself For The Self-Rejection

Forgiveness Inner Reflection of the Day

In the quiet chambers of self-discovery, I embark on a profound journey of forgiveness, seeking to release the heavy burden of self-rejection that has held me captive. I extend compassion towards myself, understanding that self-forgiveness is an act of healing and transformation.

Forgiving myself for self-rejection acknowledges that the critical voice within does not define me. My worth is innate, independent of any perceived flaws or shortcomings. Through forgiveness, I liberate myself from the chains of self-doubt and self-condemnation.

It's essential to recognize that self-rejection often stems from the echoes of past experiences and external influences. By forgiving myself, I take ownership of my narrative and reclaim the power to redefine my self-image. I release the grip of these outdated beliefs and embrace the path of self-love.

Forgiveness does not erase the pain of self-rejection but enables me to heal and grow from it. I cultivate resilience and strength through forgiveness, using my experiences as stepping stones toward self-empowerment. I learned to nurture myself with the kindness and understanding I would offer a dear friend.

Forgiving myself is an affirmation of my humanity. It's acknowledging that imperfections are an integral part of being human. By extending forgiveness, I allow space for growth and transformation. I shift from self-rejection to self-acceptance, creating an environment where I can flourish and thrive.

In the act of forgiving myself, I offer myself the gift of a fresh start. I release the weight of past mistakes and embrace the potential for change and growth. By practicing self-forgiveness, I embark on a journey of inner healing, paving the way for self-love, self-compassion, and a renewed sense of self-worth.

As I navigate this journey of self-forgiveness, I choose to release the shackles of self-rejection that have held me back. I step into the light of self-acceptance, honoring my journey and embracing the fullness of who I am. Through forgiveness, I welcome the power to heal and create a more loving and nurturing relationship with myself.

People may experience self-rejection when they internalize negative beliefs about themselves, struggle with self-esteem, or engage in self-sabotaging behaviors. This can lead to a sense of isolation and disconnection from others.

Meditative Healing Thought of the Day

I release the grip of self-rejection, gently setting it free like a bird soaring into the open sky. No longer will I allow its weight to dictate my path. Instead, I choose the path of self-compassion, where each step is fueled by self-love.

I am the author of my story, and I refuse to let self-rejection pen my narrative. Like an artist, I paint my canvas with colors of self-acceptance and kindness. With each stroke, I create a masterpiece of self-worth that radiates from within.

In the garden of my mind, I uproot the seeds of self-doubt and replace them with seeds of self-affirmation. I nurture these seeds with patience and care, watching them blossom into a self-love garden that blooms in all seasons.

My flaws or mistakes do not define me; they are mere brushstrokes that add depth to the portrait of my being. I stand firm in the face of self-rejection, knowing my worth is unwavering and unshakable.

With each breath, I inhale the essence of self-empowerment and exhale the shadows of self-doubt. I choose to walk a path illuminated by self-love, where the echoes of self-rejection fade into the distance.

I embrace my uniqueness, honoring the journey that has led me to this moment. I am a beacon of self-acceptance, and my light shines brightly for all to see. Self-rejection no longer guides me; the compass of self-love and self-belief guides me.

Deeper Connection Within

1. How can I challenge the belief that rejection defines my identity and worthiness?

_____

_____

_____

_____

_____

2. How can I build a support network of positive and like-minded individuals?

_____

_____

_____

_____

_____

3. How can I practice self-forgiveness for past decisions or actions influenced by the fear of rejection?

_____

_____

_____

_____

_____

Loving Statements About Me

I am guided by my passions and align my actions with my goals.

I believe in my ability to learn and adapt to new challenges.

I radiate positivity and inspire those around me to see their greatness.

Gratitude Reflection of the Day

I am thankful for a heart that celebrates progress over perfection. I appreciate gentle reminders that my growth is a journey, and every step forward is a reason to be grateful.

Inner Reflections

I Forgive My Employer For Denying The Promotion, Which I Took As A Rejection

Forgiveness Inner Reflection of the Day

Amid the corridors of self-discovery, I embark on a journey of forgiveness, seeking to release the weight of perceived rejection that lingers from a missed promotion. With a heart open to healing, I forgive my employer, recognizing that their decision was not a personal indictment but a part of a larger narrative.

Forgiving my employer is an act of releasing the grip of resentment that has held me captive. I acknowledge that their decision did not diminish my value or potential. By extending forgiveness, I choose to liberate myself from the cycle of self-doubt and disappointment.

In this process, I strive to understand that the decision made by my employer was a complex interplay of factors beyond my control. By choosing to forgive, I free myself from the burden of carrying the weight of perceived rejection. I recognize that my worth is not solely determined by external validation.

Through forgiveness, I embrace the opportunity to cultivate resilience and self-empowerment. I shift from dwelling on what could have been to focusing on what I can achieve moving forward. Forgiveness allows me to redirect my energy toward my personal and professional growth, unburdened by the chains of resentment.

Forgiving my employer is an act of reclaiming my power. It's acknowledging that my self-worth is not dependent on external circumstances. By extending forgiveness, I release myself from the grip of disappointment and open myself to new possibilities and opportunities.

As I navigate this journey of forgiveness, I choose to release the grasp of perceived rejection. I step into a space of self-assuredness, recognizing that my potential remains limitless despite this experience. Through forgiveness, I embrace the power to heal, grow, and create a path filled with purpose and fulfillment.

I forgive my employer for denying the promotion, which I took as a rejection.

Being denied a job opportunity, not receiving a desired promotion, or facing rejection in academic applications or scholarship opportunities can dishearten and impact one's professional or academic identity.

I forgive employers who denied my promotion.

Meditative Healing Thought of the Day

In the tapestry of my life, every instance of rejection is woven with threads of purpose and divine guidance. I release the need to view rejection as a personal failure, and instead, I embrace the truth that it is God's protection leading me towards more incredible blessings.

Just as a gardener prunes the branches to help a tree flourish, so does rejection prune my path, removing what no longer serves me and making space for the growth that lies ahead. I trust that God's plan is unfolding, even when rejection appears to divert my course.

With open arms, I welcome the lessons that rejection brings, for they lead me to more profound self-discovery and resilience. I surrender to the flow of life, knowing that what is meant for me will find its way and what is not meant for me is lovingly redirected.

Rejection is not a reflection of my worth but a redirection towards alignment with my higher purpose. I release any lingering pain or disappointment, replacing it with gratitude for the protection that rejection offers. In embracing this perspective, I step into a realm of empowerment, seeing every rejection as a step towards my destined path of fulfillment and joy.

Deeper Connection Within

1. How can I harness the power of vulnerability to connect authentically with others despite potential rejection?

_____

_____

_____

_____

_____

2. What daily practices can I adopt to reinforce my self-esteem and resilience?

_____

_____

_____

_____

_____

3. How can I redirect my focus from external validation to cultivating a deep sense of self-acceptance?

_____

_____

_____

_____

_____

Loving Statements About Me

I am resilient, and setbacks only fuel my determination to succeed.

I am a work in progress, and every step I take leads me closer to my goals.

I deserve happiness, joy, and fulfillment in all areas of my life.

Gratitude Reflection of the Day

I am thankful for guidance as I reflect on my life. I am confident in facing the future with hope, happiness, and inner peace.

Inner Reflections

DAY 12

I Forgive All Of The Romantic Rejections

Forgiveness Inner Reflection of the Day

In the realm of forgiveness, I embark on a profoundly personal journey to release the weight of all the romantic rejections that have shaped my path. With an open heart, I forgive those who turned away and myself for carrying the wounds for so long.

Forgiving all the romantic rejections is an act of self-compassion and liberation. I acknowledge that each denial was not a reflection of my worth but a part of the intricate tapestry of life's experiences. Through forgiveness, I free myself from the chains of self-doubt and insecurity these rejections left behind.

As I traverse this path, I recognize that holding onto resentment only impedes my personal growth. By extending forgiveness, I allow myself to heal and make space for new beginnings. I release the heavy burden of hurt and disappointment, allowing me to welcome love and joy into my life.

Forgiving past romantic rejections also involves forgiving myself. I choose to let go of any self-blame or feelings of inadequacy that I may have carried.

Through forgiveness, I embrace my humanity and acknowledge that imperfections are a natural part of the journey.

In this journey, I reclaim my power and agency. I am no longer defined by the rejections I've faced but by my resilience and capacity to heal. By extending forgiveness, I open myself to the possibility of attracting genuine love and meaningful connections into my life.

Reflecting on these past rejections, I let go of any lingering pain and bitterness. I acknowledge that forgiveness is a gift I give myself, a step towards emotional freedom and inner peace. Through this act of forgiveness, I release the past and create space for a brighter, more love-filled future.

Rejection in romantic relationships can take different forms, such as being turned down for a date, broken up, or experiencing unrequited love. It can be emotionally challenging and can impact one's self-esteem and confidence.

I forgive all of the romantic rejections.

Meditative Healing Thought of the Day

With an open heart, I embrace the lessons that romantic rejections bring into my life. Each rejection is a step closer to aligning with the right person, someone who sees and cherishes my essence. I release any feelings of inadequacy and replace them with a deep understanding that the right love will come at the right time.

Romantic rejections do not reflect my value or desirability; they are stepping stones toward growth and self-discovery. As I navigate relationships, I learn from each experience, gaining wisdom that guides me toward deeper connections.

I am not defined by the rejection I face but rather by my resilience and ability to continue opening my heart to love. I release self-criticism and self-doubt, recognizing that I deserve a love that uplifts and supports me.

In embracing the lessons of romantic rejections, I empower myself to seek the love that aligns with my highest good. The universe has a plan for my heart, and every rejection brings me closer to genuine, enduring, and fulfilling love.

Deeper Connection Within

1. How can I use rejection as an opportunity to expand my comfort zone and try new experiences?

_____

_____

_____

_____

_____

2. What insights can I gain from reflecting on when rejection ultimately led to positive outcomes?

_____

_____

_____

_____

_____

3. How can I transform feelings of rejection into opportunities for self-expression and creativity?

_____

_____

_____

_____

_____

Loving Statements About Me

I am open to receiving abundance from unexpected sources.

I have the power to transform my thoughts and create a positive reality.

I embrace the journey of self-discovery and continuous growth.

Gratitude Reflection of the Day

I am grateful for the gift of self-love. I can silence the inner critic and replace negative thoughts with affirmations of my worthiness and potential.

Inner Reflections

I Forgive My Children
For Their Rejection

Forgiveness Inner Reflection of the Day

In the chambers of my heart, I embark on a journey of forgiveness, seeking to liberate myself from the shackles of hurt and resentment that stem from the rejection I've experienced from my children. With each step on this path, I choose to release the heavy burden of pain and open myself to healing and understanding.

Forgiving my children for their rejection is an act of immense courage and self-love. I recognize that their actions may not stem from a lack of love but from their struggles, emotions, and perceptions. By extending forgiveness, I honor their journey and allow room for compassion to flow.

In this process, I also forgive myself for any moments of self-blame and doubt I've carried. I acknowledge that as a parent, I've done my best with the knowledge and resources I had. Through forgiveness, I release the weight of guilt and embrace the truth that no one is perfect, including myself.

By choosing to forgive, I am not condoning hurtful actions but determining my well-being over holding onto pain. Forgiving my children empowers me to regain my inner peace and allows them to grow and heal. I free myself from bitterness and resentment, allowing space for understanding and growth.

As I walk this path, I reframe my perspective. I acknowledge that forgiveness does not mean forgetting or ignoring the past but acknowledging the pain while consciously choosing to move beyond it. Extending forgiveness, I reclaim my power and create a space for open communication and healing.

I am planting the seeds of love, understanding, and healing in this journey. By forgiving my children for their rejection, I am nurturing the fertile ground for a transformed relationship, one that is built on empathy, acceptance, and growth. As I walk this path, I open my heart to the possibility of renewed connection and the joy of seeing them thrive.

I forgive my children for their rejection.

Meditative Healing Thought of the Day

In the stillness of my heart, I release the heavy burden of feeling rejected by my children. I acknowledge their actions or choices do not define my worth as a parent. Instead of clinging to the idea of rejection, I choose to see the intricate tapestry of our relationship, woven with both moments of connection and challenges.

I empower myself to shift my perspective, realizing that my children's choices reflect their journeys and experiences. I release any resentment or hurt that has built up, allowing space for understanding and compassion.

By letting go of the notion of rejection, I open myself to the possibility of healing and rebuilding bridges. I deserve love, respect, and a harmonious relationship with my children. As I release the grip of perceived rejection, I step into my power to nurture a connection based on love, empathy, and mutual growth.

Deeper Connection Within

1. How can I embrace the unknown and release the need for certainty, even in the face of rejection?

_____

_____

_____

_____

_____

2. What strategies can I implement to release past rejections and free myself from their emotional hold?

_____

_____

_____

_____

_____

3. How can I remember that the opinions of others are only a fraction of the vast spectrum of perspectives?

_____

_____

_____

_____

_____

Loving Statements About Me

I am confident in my ability to handle any obstacles that come my way.

I am committed to nurturing my mind, body, and soul for holistic success.

I create opportunities and take bold actions toward my goals.

Gratitude Reflection of the Day

I am thankful for the strength to release the weight of past mistakes. I am courageous to let go of regrets and embrace the freedom of a new beginning.

Inner Reflections

I Forgive Any Teachers Who Belittled & Insulted Me

Forgiveness Inner Reflection of the Day

Amid the corridors of my soul, I embark on a journey of forgiveness aimed at liberating myself from the weight of hurt and humiliation inflicted by teachers who belittled and insulted me. Through forgiveness, I choose to release the grip of resentment and create space for healing and growth.

Forgiving the teachers who have wounded me is an act of self-compassion and strength. I acknowledge that their actions may have been driven by their insecurities, biases, or limitations. I rise above their hurtful words by extending forgiveness and embracing my worth.

In this process, I also forgive myself for carrying the burden of those hurtful experiences. I release the self-doubt and internalized negativity that may have resulted from their actions. Through forgiveness, I reclaim my sense of self and remind myself that I deserve respect and dignity.

By choosing to forgive, I am not absolving them of their behavior but freeing myself from the chains of anger and bitterness. Forgiving the teachers who belittled and insulted me empowers me to reclaim my voice and confidence. I acknowledge that their opinions do not determine my worth.

In this journey, I reshaped my perspective. I recognize that forgiveness is not an endorsement of their actions but a declaration of my inner strength. By extending forgiveness, I release their words' hold on me and create space for healing and empowerment.

As I walk this path of forgiveness, I plant the seeds of self-love, resilience, and growth. By forgiving the teachers who hurt me, I cultivate an environment of self-acceptance and positivity within myself. I rise above the past through forgiveness and move toward a future filled with self-assuredness and joy.

I forgive teachers who rejected and belittled me.

Meditative Healing Thought of the Day

In the quiet corners of my mind, I release the echoes of past belittlement by teachers. I understand that their words reflected their limitations, not a measure of my potential. I reclaim my inner strength and self-assurance, knowing I can achieve greatness.

I embrace the journey of learning and growth, knowing that the opinions of others do not determine my worth. The scars of their words fade as I replace them with affirmations of my abilities and resilience.

I choose to stand tall, guided by my inner wisdom and determination.

With each step, I empower myself to rise above the shadows of doubt and insecurity. I am confident in my abilities and the unique path I am forging. The teacher's belittlement no longer defines me; my resilience, courage, and unwavering belief in my potential determine me.

Deeper Connection Within

1. How can I cultivate self-love and self-compassion as foundations for resilience against rejection?

_____

_____

_____

_____

_____

2. How can I reframe rejection as a chance to redirect my path and pursue more aligned opportunities?

_____

_____

_____

_____

_____

3. What steps can I take to focus on my personal growth and development, regardless of external opinions?

_____

_____

_____

_____

_____

Loving Statements About Me

I trust myself to make the right choices that align with my vision.

I am worthy of achieving my dreams and willing to put in the effort.

I release fear and doubt, allowing my inner strength to shine through.

Gratitude Reflection of the Day

I recognize that I am a beautiful masterpiece made with love. I welcome joy while celebrating my individuality and intentionally live a purposeful life.

Inner Reflections

I Forgive People Online For Their Harsh Judgment And Rejection

Forgiveness Inner Reflection of the Day

In the vast expanse of the digital world, I embark on a journey of forgiveness, aiming to release the weight of harsh judgment and rejection inflicted by people online. Through forgiveness, I seek to liberate myself from the burden of their hurtful words and rekindle my sense of self-worth.

Forgiving those who have subjected me to online criticism is an act of reclaiming my power and resilience. I acknowledge that their words may be fueled by their insecurities or lack of understanding. I rise above their negativity by extending forgiveness and protecting my inner peace.

Furthermore, I extend forgiveness to myself for internalizing the judgments and feeling hurt by the rejection. Through this process, I release the self-doubt and vulnerability that their words may have triggered. By forgiving myself, I reaffirm my values and right to a positive online experience.

Forgiveness does not mean condoning their behavior but rather freeing myself from the shackles of resentment. In choosing to forgive, I embrace the possibility of growth and healing. I am reclaiming my digital space, where the opinions of others do not dictate my self-esteem.

This journey allows me to transform my perception. Forgiving those who have judged and rejected me online empowers me to shift my focus from negativity to my well-being. By extending forgiveness, I invite compassion into my heart and nurture a space for personal growth and emotional resilience.

As I navigate this path of forgiveness, I plant the seeds of self-compassion and authenticity. By forgiving the online critics, I cultivate an environment of self-love and acceptance within myself. Through forgiveness, I reclaim my sense of identity and move forward with the knowledge that my worth is not defined by the opinions of strangers on the internet.

With the prevalence of social media and online communities, individuals can experience rejection through cyberbullying, online harassment, or the adverse reactions of others to their posts, opinions, or personal information shared online.

I forgive the harsh judgment and rejection from people online.

Meditative Healing Thought of the Day

In the realm of cyberspace, I find the strength to shield my spirit from the arrows of online judgment and criticism. I remember that their words merely reflect their insecurities and biases, not an accurate measure of my worth.

I rise above the noise, holding onto the core of my authenticity and self-belief. Their negativity cannot extinguish the light within me. With a heart of resilience, I navigate this digital landscape, allowing only positivity and constructive feedback to shape my growth.

As I walk this path, I am empowered to let go of the weight of virtual opinions. I focus on cultivating connections that uplift and inspire while dismissing the rest with a gracious detachment. My worth is not tied to strangers' views, and I can forge my path without hesitation or fear.

In the silence of my inner sanctuary, I find solace. The judgment of others loses its grip as I anchor myself in my self-assuredness. I continue to share my voice, talents, and passions with the world, unaffected by the transient winds of online judgment.

Deeper Connection Within

1. How can I celebrate my achievements and progress instead of measuring success based on external validation?

_____

_____

_____

_____

_____

2. How can I turn moments of rejection into opportunities to practice empathy and understanding?

_____

_____

_____

_____

_____

3. What daily practices can help me cultivate a resilient, positive mindset in the face of rejection?

_____

_____

_____

_____

_____

Loving Statements About Me

I am a magnet for success and attract positivity into my life.

I am resilient and view challenges as stepping stones to my greatness.

I am open to embracing new experiences that enrich my journey.

Gratitude Reflection of the Day

I am so thankful for my journey through life thus far. Navigating forward with the confidence to face challenges head-on and the humility to acknowledge my growth with gratitude.

Inner Reflections

I Forgive Those Who Reject Me Due To Their Prejudices

Forgiveness Inner Reflection of the Day

Embarking on a journey of forgiveness, I navigate the complex territory of releasing the pain caused by those who reject me due to their prejudices. Through forgiveness, I aim to liberate myself from the weight of their bias and reclaim my sense of self-worth.

Forgiving those who harbor prejudices empowers me to rise above their limited perspectives. I recognize that their rejection is rooted in their biases, which often have nothing to do with my inherent values. By extending forgiveness, I release the grip of their opinions on my self-esteem.

Furthermore, I extend forgiveness to myself for internalizing their rejection. In doing so, I let go of any self-doubt or feelings of inadequacy that their prejudices may have triggered. Through self-forgiveness, I reaffirm my worth and acknowledge that I deserve respect and acceptance.

Forgiveness doesn't negate the harm caused by their prejudice; rather, it frees me from carrying the burden of their narrow-mindedness. In choosing forgiveness,

I am choosing to prioritize my emotional well-being and growth. I'm reclaiming the power to define myself beyond the confines of their biases.

As I navigate this journey, I'm cultivating compassion within myself. By forgiving those who reject me due to their prejudices, I am choosing to break the negativity cycle and foster a space of understanding. I'm laying the foundation for inner peace and personal growth through forgiveness.

This path of forgiveness is not about condoning their behavior but rather about releasing myself from the grip of their prejudice. By forgiving, I'm embracing the opportunity to heal and grow beyond the pain of rejection. I'm reminding myself that the biases of others do not determine my worth; it is inherent and unshakable.

In this process, I'm reclaiming my sense of identity and self-worth, detaching from the limitations of others' prejudices. I'm nurturing my well-being through forgiveness and creating space for a brighter, more inclusive future.

I forgive those who reject me due to their prejudices.

Meditative Healing Thought of the Day

In the face of ignorance and prejudgment, I stand tall in the sanctuary of my truth. Their limited perspectives and biases do not define me or my worth. I am a canvas painted with the hues of diversity, and their inability to see beyond their preconceptions reflects their limitations, not mine.

I choose to rise above the weight of their assumptions, embracing the power of self-awareness and education. Through my actions and words, I become a beacon of understanding, dismantling stereotypes and fostering empathy.

As I walk this path, I am empowered to let go of the burden of seeking validation from those who cannot see the richness of my identity. I recognize that their judgments stem from their narrow lenses, and I refuse to be confined by their perceptions.

In the realm of my authenticity, I find refuge. Their prejudgments lose their potency as I grow, evolve, and educate myself. I extend compassion to their lack of understanding while nurturing my self-worth, unshaken by their biases.

I navigate life gracefully, understanding that their ignorance is not my burden. With each step, I forge my path and shape my narrative, a narrative that transcends their limited vision and embraces the mosaic of my being.

Deeper Connection Within

1. How can I embrace rejection as a catalyst for growth, acknowledging that change often involves discomfort?

_____

_____

_____

_____

_____

2. How can I remind myself that I am not defined by the opinions of others but by my inner strength?

_____

_____

_____

_____

_____

3. How can I redirect my energy from dwelling on past rejections to investing in present and future pursuits?

_____

_____

_____

_____

_____

Loving Statements About Me

I believe in my potential to make a meaningful impact in the world.

I am confident in my abilities to overcome obstacles and thrive.

I am worthy of all the blessings that come my way, big and small.

Gratitude Reflection of the Day

I am thankful for the lessons learned from my past experiences. I will use them as stepping stones to greater understanding, compassion, and self-love.

Inner Reflections

I Forgive Those Who Reject My Loved Ones

Forgiveness Inner Reflection of the Day

Delving into the realm of forgiveness, I find myself grappling with the act of forgiving those who have rejected my loved ones. It's a journey that requires empathy, understanding, and a conscious effort to rise above the hurt.

Forgiveness in this context means acknowledging that everyone has their journey and perspectives. It's about releasing the grip of anger and resentment that can arise from witnessing the rejection of those close to me. By forgiving, I free myself from the emotional burden of their actions.

I recognize that people's choices are often influenced by their experiences, fears, and biases. Forgiving them doesn't excuse their behavior, but it allows me to let go of the negative energy that can fester within me. It's a step toward inner peace and emotional healing.

In forgiving those who reject my loved ones, I'm also acknowledging that I cannot control the actions or opinions of others. Instead of dwelling on their rejection, I'm focusing on supporting and uplifting my loved ones in their journey.

Additionally, I extend forgiveness to myself for any resentment or bitterness that may have arisen due to these rejections. It's an opportunity to cultivate self-compassion and acknowledge that my feelings are valid. By letting go of negative emotions, I create space for healing and growth within myself.

Forgiveness doesn't mean forgetting or condoning hurtful actions. Instead, it's a conscious decision to release rejection's hold on my heart. It's a step toward emotional liberation and directing my energy toward positive connections and experiences.

Through forgiveness, I'm creating a ripple effect of healing. I am contributing to a more compassionate world by showing compassion and understanding. While I may not change the minds of those who have rejected my loved ones, I can change how I respond and the energy I bring into my life.

As I reflect on this journey, I am reminded that forgiveness is a gift I give to myself. It's an opportunity to rise above negativity, release emotional burdens, and cultivate peace. I'm creating space for love, healing, and growth to flourish by forgiving those who reject my loved ones.

I forgive those who reject my loved ones.

Meditative Healing Thought of the Day

In the tapestry of life, every thread holds its own story. As I encounter those who reject my loved ones, I remind myself that their actions are shaped by their experiences, fears, and perspectives. Just as I seek understanding and empathy, I extend the same compassion to them.

Instead of allowing judgment to cloud my thoughts, I choose to be a source of support for my loved ones. I stand by them with unwavering love and compassion, knowing that my role is to uplift and empower, not engage in the negativity cycle.

Through this healing journey, I release the need to internalize their rejection. Their choices do not diminish the worth or significance of my loved ones. I focus on fostering a positive and nurturing environment for those I care about, showing them they are cherished and valued.

By rising above the impulse to judge, I free myself from the weight of negativity and resentment. I become a beacon of strength and support, offering a safe haven for my loved ones to flourish. In doing so, I cultivate a love, understanding, and unity space that transcends rejection boundaries.

Deeper Connection Within

1. What steps can I take to release the need for perfectionism and allow myself to be imperfectly human?

_____

_____

_____

_____

_____

2. How can I recognize rejection as a universal experience, and I am not alone in facing it?

_____

_____

_____

_____

_____

3. How can I turn rejection into a source of inspiration to challenge myself and surpass my expectations?

_____

_____

_____

_____

_____

Loving Statements About Me

I trust the process of life and know that everything unfolds in divine timing.

I am worthy of self-love, self-care, and unshakeable self-belief.

I am the captain of my ship, steering my life towards success and fulfillment.

Gratitude Reflection of the Day

I am grateful for the courage to stand firm in my identity, even when faced with the opinions of others. Unconditionally, self-love is helping me celebrate who I am.

Inner Reflections

I Forgive Those Who Reject & Undermine My Femininity

Forgiveness Inner Reflection of the Day

Forgiving those who reject and undermine my femininity is a profound journey of self-empowerment and healing. It's a process that allows me to rise above societal expectations and embrace my authentic self with compassion and strength.

Forgiveness in this context means acknowledging the impact of societal norms and conditioning on people's perceptions. It's about understanding that their rejection or belittlement often stems from their insecurities and biases. By forgiving, I release myself from the shackles of their judgment and negativity.

In forgiving those who undermine my femininity, I'm also acknowledging my worth and embracing the diversity of femininity. Instead of seeking validation from external sources, I'm learning to validate and appreciate myself for who I am. It's a step toward reclaiming my power and self-confidence.

Additionally, I extend forgiveness to myself for any moments of self-doubt or internalized negativity due to external rejection. It's an opportunity to practice self-love and remind myself that others' opinions do not define my femininity. By letting go of self-criticism, I open the door to self-acceptance and self-celebration.

Forgiveness doesn't mean accepting or conforming to others' opinions; it's a declaration of my autonomy. It's a conscious choice to release the weight of others' views and embrace my femininity on my terms. It's an act of liberation and empowerment.

Through forgiveness, I'm also challenging societal norms and contributing to a more inclusive world. I'm disrupting the cycle of judgment and negativity by showing compassion to those who reject or belittle femininity. It's a radical act of self-love and social progress.

Reflecting on this journey, I am reminded that forgiveness is an act of courage and self-compassion. It's a way of honoring my authentic self, regardless of others' opinions. By forgiving those who reject and undermine my femininity, I'm embracing a path of empowerment, self-love, and transformation.

I forgive those who reject and undermine my femininity.

Meditative Healing Thought of the Day

In the radiant light of self-love, I embrace my femininity with unwavering confidence. I rise above the opinions and actions of those who seek to undermine it, knowing that my strength lies in my authenticity. Their words and judgments cannot define my worth or shape my identity.

With each step I take, I embody the power of my femininity with grace and boldness. I stand tall, knowing my strength is not determined by conforming to others' expectations. I choose to celebrate my uniqueness and embrace the richness of my femininity.

As I navigate this journey, I surround myself with those who uplift and honor my essence. Their support and encouragement become a shield against the negativity of those who seek to diminish me. I carry myself confidently, knowing that my femininity is a source of empowerment, not vulnerability.

With each moment of self-assuredness, I send ripples of empowerment into the world. I inspire others to embrace their authentic selves and rise above the judgments of others. Through my resilience and boldness, I break free from the chains of others' opinions and stand firmly in my light.

During challenges, I hold onto the truth that my femininity is a source of strength, resilience, and beauty. I release the need to seek validation from those who undermine it, and instead, I flourish in my self-acceptance.

Deeper Connection Within

1. How can I foster self-compassion and self-care as anchors during perceived rejection?

_____

_____

_____

_____

_____

2. What empowering stories and role models can I draw inspiration from when facing rejection?

_____

_____

_____

_____

_____

3. How can I remind myself that my worth is inherent and not dependent on external validation?

_____

_____

_____

_____

_____

Loving Statements About Me

I am resilient and bounce back stronger from any setbacks I encounter.

I release self-sabotaging thoughts and replace them with empowering beliefs.

I am open to receiving help and support as I pursue my dreams.

Gratitude Reflection of the Day

I am grateful for confidence and self-motivation. I radiate self-assurance and inspire myself and others to embrace their uniqueness.

Inner Reflections

DAY 19

I Forgive The Rejection
Motherhood Brings

Forgiveness Inner Reflection of the Day

Forgiving the rejection that motherhood sometimes brings is a profound act of self-compassion and growth. It's a process that requires acknowledging the challenges, embracing imperfections, and finding strength within oneself.

Forgiveness in this context involves letting go of the expectations we might have had about motherhood. It means releasing the pressure to meet societal ideals and accepting that no one has all the answers. It's recognizing that rejection of our efforts doesn't define our worth as mothers.

By forgiving the moments of self-doubt, exhaustion, and frustration that motherhood can bring, we free ourselves from the heavy burden of perfectionism. It's a way to cultivate self-love and nurture a resilient spirit. Forgiveness allows us to move forward with grace and understanding for ourselves and our children.

Moreover, forgiving the challenges of motherhood means acknowledging that rejection doesn't equate to failure. It's recognizing that the journey is filled with ups and downs and that rejection is a part of the learning process. It's a chance to reframe rejection as an opportunity for growth and transformation.

Forgiving the rejection motherhood brings also involves releasing comparisons with others. Each mother's journey is unique, and embracing this diversity allows us to focus on our path without constantly measuring ourselves against others. It's a powerful way to cultivate self-acceptance and inner peace.

As we reflect on this journey of forgiveness, we learn that it's not about denying the difficulties but transforming our relationship with them. By forgiving the rejection that motherhood sometimes brings, we create space for love, gratitude, and joy to flourish. We allow ourselves to fully experience the beauty and challenges of raising children.

In forgiving the rejection motherhood brings, we honor our strength, resilience, and capacity to love. We recognize imperfections don't define us as mothers but make us beautifully human. Through this forgiveness, we embrace the fullness of the motherhood experience and embark on a path of self-discovery and growth.

I forgive the rejection motherhood brings.

Meditative Healing Thought of the Day

I find the strength to thrive in the heart of motherhood's challenges. Every rejection and setback only fuels my determination to become a better parent. I release the weight of perfection and embrace the journey of growth.

I rise above the doubts and criticisms, knowing that my love and efforts are valuable and worthy. I stand firm in the face of rejection, using it as a stepping stone to cultivate resilience. Through the highs and lows, I remain committed to the well-being of my children.

Rejection is an opportunity for growth, a chance to reflect on my approach and make positive changes. I refuse to let it define my worth or role as a mother. Instead, I use it as a catalyst to become more compassionate, patient, and understanding.

Amid rejection, I find moments of connection and joy that remind me of the beauty of motherhood. I celebrate the small victories and milestones, knowing they outweigh the challenges. I focus on the love I give and receive and let it guide me through the journey.

As I navigate the complexities of motherhood, I draw strength from within and from the support of those who uplift me. I am a resilient and nurturing mother, capable of thriving despite the rejection that may come my way. My love is my foundation, and it empowers me to push through, evolve, and create a beautiful and meaningful journey for my children.

Deeper Connection Within

1. How can I embrace rejection as a natural part of life without allowing it to define my self-worth?

_____

_____

_____

_____

_____

2. What practices can I integrate into my daily routine to cultivate resilience and inner strength?

_____

_____

_____

_____

_____

3. How can I reframe rejection as a stepping stone on the path towards my unique journey?

_____

_____

_____

_____

_____

Loving Statements About Me

I believe in my talents, skills, and unique gifts that set me apart.

I control my destiny and make choices that lead to my desired outcomes.

I am confident in my ability to overcome challenges and rise above adversity.

Gratitude Reflection of the Day

I am thankful for the strength to release comparison and self-criticism. I can embrace my journey and confidently walk my path of inner healing and peace.

Inner Reflections

DAY 20

I Forgive Those Who Reject My Existence

Forgiveness Inner Reflection of the Day

Forgiving those who reject my existence is a transformative journey that leads to personal liberation and inner peace. It's a process of releasing the weight of their opinions and finding strength within my self-worth.

Forgiveness here involves acknowledging that the rejection from others is often a reflection of their insecurities, biases, or misunderstandings. By forgiving them, I am not condoning their behavior but freeing myself from the burden of carrying their judgments.

Forgiving those who reject my existence allows me to reclaim my power and define my worth on my terms. It means recognizing that their opinions do not represent who I am. It's about cultivating self-love and confidence from within, irrespective of external validation.

Through this inner reflection, I understand that my existence is valuable and worthy, regardless of others' perceptions. Forgiveness helps me let go of the pain

169

that rejection can bring and instead embrace a sense of freedom to be authentic and unapologetic.

Moreover, forgiving those who reject my existence creates space for empathy and compassion. It enables me to see them as flawed individuals with their struggles and fears. It doesn't excuse their behavior, but it allows me to move forward with a sense of grace and understanding.

In forgiving those who reject my existence, I release the emotional ties that bind me to their opinions. I reclaim my narrative and create a new self-acceptance, growth, and resilience story. It's a step towards building a life aligned with my values and aspirations rather than being defined by others' judgments.

Ultimately, forgiveness in this context is an act of self-love and empowerment. It's a decision to honor my worthiness, regardless of external rejection. Through this inner transformation, I can embrace my existence with a newfound sense of purpose and authenticity, unburdened by the opinions of others.

I forgive those who reject my existence.

Meditative Healing Thought of the Day

I am more than the judgments of others; I am a unique and valuable individual. I embrace my existence and find strength in self-love. The opinions of those who reject me do not define my worth.

I focus on my growth, happiness, and well-being, nurturing my love for myself. Through self-compassion, I rise above the pain of rejection, knowing that I deserve acceptance and respect. I stand firm in my authenticity, unapologetically shining as I am. I release the burden of seeking validation from those who do not understand me, and I choose to surround myself with positivity and support.

My journey is a tapestry of experiences; I am the artist who shapes its colors and patterns. I embrace my existence with grace, knowing that my self-love empowers me to overcome rejection and find fulfillment from within.

Deeper Connection Within

1. How can I find solace in the realization that the people who reject me may not honestly know me?

_____

_____

_____

_____

_____

2. How can I detach my self-worth from external validation and anchor it in my self-perception?

_____

_____

_____

_____

_____

3. What steps can I take to release the need to control others' opinions of me and focus on my growth?

_____

_____

_____

_____

_____

Loving Statements About Me

I am worthy of achieving my goals and living a life filled with purpose.

I trust that every experience, whether positive or negative, contributes to my growth.

I am capable of achieving greatness, and I embrace opportunities to shine.

Gratitude Reflection of the Day

I am thankful for the humility to recognize that my worth comes from within me.

Joy fills my soul when I remember that I am always worthy of celebrating my accomplishments.

Inner Reflections

DAY 21

I Forgive Those Who Reject Me Due To The Melanin In My Skin

Forgiveness Inner Reflection of the Day

Forgiving those who reject me due to my skin color is a profound act of healing and self-empowerment. It involves confronting the pain of racial discrimination and releasing its hold on my heart and mind.

Forgiveness in this context is not about condoning or excusing the hurtful behavior of others. It's about reclaiming my sense of worth and refusing to let their prejudice define my self-concept. It's acknowledging that their rejection is rooted in their ignorance and biases.

Through this inner insight, I recognize that their rejection reflects their limited perspective rather than a reflection of my value as a human being. Forgiving them allows me to detach from the hurtful words and actions and instead embrace a sense of empowerment.

Forgiving those who reject me due to the melanin in my skin means breaking free from the chains of internalized oppression. It means recognizing that their opinions do not determine my self-worth. By choosing to forgive, I declare that I am more than the color of my skin—I am a person of value and significance.

Furthermore, forgiveness enables me to shift my focus from seeking validation from those who reject me to embracing the love and support of those who uplift and affirm me. It allows me to channel my energy into creating change, advocating for justice, and fostering a sense of unity among all people.

Forgiving those who reject me due to my skin color is a radical act of self-love and resistance. It's a declaration that I will not be defined by the ignorance of others but by my strength, resilience, and potential. It's a step towards healing from the wounds of racism and building a future where everyone is valued and respected, regardless of skin color.

Meditative Healing Thought of the Day

The richness of my melanin is a badge of honor, a symbol of heritage and strength. I pridefully embrace my skin, knowing its beauty holds stories of resilience and history.

I stand tall and unapologetic, radiating confidence from the core of my being. The opinions of those who fail to recognize the power in my melanin hold no weight against the self-assured glow that emanates from within.

I am a masterpiece of diversity, a reflection of the countless shades that make up the tapestry of humanity. I celebrate the uniqueness of my skin and the identity it represents.

With each step, I leave a mark of self-love and empowerment, shattering the barriers of prejudice and ignorance. I am bold, I am beautiful, and I am unstoppable.

Deeper Connection Within

1. How can I channel my energy into positive outlets that allow me to express myself authentically?

_____

_____

_____

_____

_____

2. How can I embrace rejection as a chance to build emotional resilience and cultivate a strong sense of self?

_____

_____

_____

_____

_____

3. What daily intentions can I set to remind myself that I am enough, regardless of perceived rejections?

_____

_____

_____

_____

_____

Loving Statements About Me

I deserve success, happiness, and all the good things life offers.

I am resilient and continue to push forward, even when faced with obstacles.

I believe in myself and my potential to create a life that reflects my true essence.

Gratitude Reflection of the Day

I am grateful for the unconditional love, prosperity, and favor I've received. I will always celebrate the person I was created to be and find joy in living an abundant life.

Inner Reflections

Story Time

O nce upon a time in a bustling city, there lived a woman named Heather. On the surface, she seemed to have it all— a successful career, a loving family, and a circle of friends who admired her. But beneath the façade of success and contentment, Heather carried a heavy burden. She had spent most of her life trying to meet the expectations of others, constantly seeking external validation.

Heather's journey towards empowerment and authenticity began one crisp autumn morning when she stumbled upon a journal in a quaint bookstore. Its title, "Forgiving People Who Reject You," caught her eye. Heather decided to purchase the journal, thinking it might offer some temporary solace to her restless soul.

As she delved into the pages, Heather discovered a treasure trove of wisdom. The journal encouraged introspection and self-discovery, urging readers to shed the masks they wore and embrace their true selves. It was a revelation for Heather, and she decided to embark on a journey of self-empowerment.

Her first step was to seek therapy to unravel the layers of her past that had led her to constantly seek validation. Through therapy, she uncovered childhood experiences that had left her feeling unworthy and unlovable. Heather realized that the opinions of others had never defined her worth, and she could choose to embrace her authenticity.

She began practicing self-compassion and self-acceptance. Heather started setting boundaries with people who had taken advantage of her eagerness to please. It was not easy, and she faced resistance from those who were accustomed to her compliance. However, Heather was determined to live life on her terms.

In her personal and professional life, she started speaking her truth. She shared her dreams, her desires, and her vulnerabilities openly. Some relationships fell by the wayside as people couldn't accept the new, empowered Heather. But others grew deeper as they appreciated her authenticity.

As Heather continued on her journey, she noticed profound changes in herself. Her body felt lighter, and she radiated confidence and self-assuredness. Her mind was free from the constant chatter of self-doubt, and her soul was at peace.

Heather's transformation was not just physical; it was a complete shift in mindset and spirit. She had embraced empowerment and authenticity as her guiding principles, and they had reshaped her life in ways she could have never imagined.

Heather's story became an inspiration to others who were trapped in the same cycle of seeking external validation. She became a beacon of hope, showing them that the path to true fulfillment and happiness began with self-empowerment and embracing one's authentic self. Heather's journey had transformed her life mind, body, and soul, and it was a testament to the incredible power of authenticity and empowerment.

Embracing E & A

As you close the pages of this journal, take a moment to reflect on the remarkable journey you've undertaken. It's a journey that begins with acknowledging and facing the feelings of rejection and abandonment that have weighed heavily on your heart. You've shown immense courage in confronting these emotions, and your commitment to healing and transformation has been truly inspiring.

Throughout this journal, you've explored the depths of your emotions, delved into your past experiences, and bravely questioned the patterns that have shaped your thoughts and actions. You've shed light on the wounds often hidden beneath the surface, and through your introspection, you've started to release their hold on your heart and mind.

As you've navigated the intricate layers of your feelings, you've come to understand that rejection and abandonment do not reflect your worth. They are the byproducts of others' limitations, misconceptions, and struggles. In realizing this, you've begun to untangle the web of self-doubt and self-criticism that these feelings have woven.

But your journey doesn't end here; it's a stepping stone to a more extraordinary transformation. As you complete this journal, embrace the empowerment of choosing self-compassion over self-judgment—

the empowerment to stand tall in your authenticity, unapologetically embracing every facet of your being.

You've embarked on a path toward joy, kindness, and authenticity. With every step, you've built a bridge between your past and your future, paving the way for a life where self-love and acceptance are the cornerstones. As you move forward, remember that you can rewrite your narrative. Embrace the lessons you've learned, but do not let them define you. Let them inspire you to live your life on your terms.

In this transformation, practice kindness – both towards yourself and others. Cultivate a heart that understands the struggles and complexities each individual carries. Your journey has given you the insight to recognize that we are all fighting battles that others might not see. Extend compassion and understanding, for you know firsthand the healing power it holds.

As you venture into the world with your newfound authenticity, radiate joy from within. Surround yourself with positivity, foster relationships that uplift your spirit, and engage in activities that resonate with your passions. Remember, joy is not just a fleeting emotion; it's a state of being you can choose daily.

This closing chapter is not an end but a continuation of the remarkable journey you've embarked upon. Carry the lessons, the self-compassion, and the empowerment with you as you step into the future. Know that your transformation has ripple effects

– inspiring those around you to embrace their authenticity, to let go of the shackles of rejection, and to rise into their true selves.

You are a testament to the resilience of the human spirit. Your willingness to confront your past, heal your wounds, and transform your narrative is a powerful reminder that we can overcome even the deepest pains. As you turn the page to the next chapter of your life, go forth with unwavering faith in your ability to rise, thrive, and live authentically, empowered, and beautifully.

With heartfelt gratitude for sharing your journey within these pages,

Tuniscia O

WRITE A LETTER TO YOUR FUTURE SELF ABOUT HOW YOUR LIFE TRANSFORMED ONCE YOU STARTED TO LOVE YOURSELF MORE THAN THE APPROVAL OF OTHERS

_____

_____

_____

_____

_____

_____

_____

_____

_____

_____

_____

_____

_____

_____

_____

_____

_____

_____

_____

_____

_____

_____

_____

Below Is A List Of All 35 Forgiveness Journals

Written By: Tuniscia Okeke

Available on Amazon and other major bookstores or www.forgivenesslifestyle.com
Instagram: @forgivenesslifestyle
For bulk orders: info@forgivenesslifestyle.com

Forgiving Yourself

Forgiving Your Body Journal

Accepting the Gift of Forgiveness Journal

Forgiving People Who Reject You Journal

P.S. Forgive Yourself First Journal

Who Do You Struggle To Forgive Journal

Forgiving Your Struggle With Addiction Journal

Parenthood

Forgiving and Overcoming Mom Guilt Journal

Forgiveness Journal for Fathers

Parents Forgiving Tweens/Teen Journal

Parents Forgiving Adult Children Journal

Forgiving Your Parents

Forgiving Your Mother Journal

Forgiving Your Father Journal

Forgiving Your Parents Journal

Family

Forgiving Dead Loved One's Journal

Forgiving Family Secrets Journal

Forgiving The Bullies In Your Family Journal

Forgiving Your Siblings Journal

Marriage

Forgiving Your Wife Journal
Forgiving Your Husband Journal
Forgiving Your Mother-
In-Law Journal

Romantic Relationships

Forgiving Your Ex Journal
Forgiving The "New"
Woman Journal

Teens & Millennials

Forgiveness Journals for Teens
Forgiveness Journal
for Millennials

Religion

Forgiving God Journal
Forgiving Church People Journal

Blended Family

Forgiving A Co-Parent Journal
Forgiveness Journal
for Stepmothers
Forgiving Your
Stepmother Journal
Forgiving Your Stepkids
Mom Journal

Relationships

Forgiving Your Abuser Journal
Forgiving Friends Journal

Business/Finances

Forgiveness In Business Journal
Forgiving People At
Work Journal
Forgiving Past Money
Mistakes Journal

Sending you loving energy as you
forgive, heal, and grow.
www.forgivenesslifestyle.com

Thank You

Gratitude is the thread that weaves connections, and at this moment, I extend my deepest appreciation to those whose unwavering support and love have been the foundation of this 35-journal writing journey and beyond.

To my beloved husband, your unwavering confidence and support during our marriage and this writing project have been my anchor. Thank you for your belief in me. It has been a constant source of inspiration. Your love and presence in my life make my soul smile.

To my mother, your honesty and vulnerability have led to this beautiful healing journey. Your transparency has supported my healing and given me the strength to support others on their transformational journey. I will forever be grateful for your courage to tell the truth.

My dear daughter, Shantia Dajah, your reminder to give myself grace has been a guiding light. Your wisdom transcends your years. You make my heart smile.

To my incredible son, Damien, your encouragement and motivation have fueled my determination to embark on this transformative journey. Your presence in my life is a source of boundless joy.

To Ike, my dynamic youngest son, your cheering from the sidelines has been a source of motivation and warmth. Your enthusiasm lights up my days.

My sister, Tanniedra, your unwavering belief in me and our brainstorming sessions have been invaluable. You are truly a gift.

Little sister, Jazmin, your willingness to share your experiences and vulnerability has touched my heart deeply. Your courage is inspiring.

To my "business bestie," Martha Banks Hall, the Creator of Vision Words, your prayers, encouraging texts, and our deep explorations of thoughts have been a source of clarity and growth to help me birth this project.

Denise, my beautiful friend, "The Fertility Godmother," your enthusiastic voice memos have made me feel like a rock star. Your presence has been a pillar of my strength.

To Thuy, I'm deeply grateful for your accountability and sisterhood, and I hold you as the beautiful gift you are close to my heart.

To Georgette and Cristal, your cheers have lifted my spirits. Your presence in my life is a blessing.

You all hold a special place in my heart, and I thank you from the depths of my soul for being a part of my journey.

Made in the USA
Middletown, DE
15 October 2023

40779090R00116